Stand Your Ground—
TO KILL, OR NOT TO KILL...
The Legal Limits of Safety

by
Jack Forbes

© 2012 Jack Forbes

Stand Your Ground —
TO KILL, OR NOT TO KILL...
The Legal Limits of Safety

by
Jack Forbes

Copyright ©2012 by Jack Forbes

ISBN 978-0-9836418-5-8

Published by
JAFO PUBLISHING
375 Redondo Avenue
PMB 320
Long Beach, California 90814

All rights are reserved, but for permitted use by the U.S. Copyright Act of 1976. No part of this publication may be distributed, reproduced, stored or transmitted in any form or by any means electronic or mechanical, or by any information storage or retrieval system without the prior written permission of the copyright owner.

Printed in the United States of America

Book Design—Typography—Cover Design—Retouching
M. Redmond — Redmond & Associates
Specialty: Designer ePub, Mobi & Programing—R. Korns
www.marioncreative.com   rkorns@worthgold.com

Contact Information:
www.JafoPublishing.com

TABLE OF CONTENTS

DEDICATION 1

ACKNOWLEDGEMENTS 3

PROLOGUE 4

OVERVIEW 12

SCENARIO #1 Basic Self-defense 27

SCENARIO #2 30
Fear of assault or battery not rising to the level
of bodily harm

SCENARIO #3 35
Deadly force and the defense of others

SCENARIO #4 40
Actual harm versus perceived harm

SCENARIO #5 Mutual combat 51

Stand Your Ground—
TO KILL, OR NOT TO KILL...

TABLE OF CONTENTS

SCENARIO #6 58
Imminent harm, defense of others

SCENARIO #7 64
Reasonable force, withdrawal from the fight

SCENARIO #8 75
Battered person syndrome, imminent harm

SCENARIO #9 81
Actual harm versus perceived harm, defense of others

SCENARIO #10 87
Defense of property, deadly force

SCENARIO #11 102
No duty to retreat

SCENARIO #12 112
Wrongdoers

TABLE OF CONTENTS

SCENARIO #13 120
Mutual combat, escalation of force

SCENARIO #14 125
Defense of others, no duty to retreat

SCENARIO #15 132
Imminent harm

SCENARIO #16 138
Sudden and deadly counterassault, duty to retreat

SCENARIO #17 145
Imminent harm, reasonable belief

SCENARIO #18 149
Excessive force by a peace officer

SCENARIO #19 154
Alcohol and mental illness

Stand Your Ground—
TO KILL, OR NOT TO KILL...

TABLE OF CONTENTS

SCENARIO #20 159
Transferred intent

CONCLUDING OBSERVATIONS 162

APPENDIX 164

DEDICATION

This writing is dedicated to my loving sister Ginger, whose life was cut short by the cowardly and brutal acts of two individuals over 30 years ago. The memory of Ginger's life and of her courage gives me strength. The joy of life gives me purpose. The desire to protect other potential victims gives me resolve.

Stand Your Ground—
TO KILL, OR NOT TO KILL...
The Legal Limits of Safety

ACKNOWLEDGEMENTS

I would not be a Black Belt in Chinese Kenpo Karate, were it not for my instructor, 7th Degree Black Belt David Brock. David won eight black belt International Fighting Champion titles and also won a title as the U.S.A. National Self-defense Champion. In 1999, David was inducted into the Black Belt Hall of Fame.

David selflessly took me under his wing, inspired me with his own extraordinary accomplishments, talents and aspirations, and pushed me to excel as a martial artist. David is pictured on the back cover with me.

Stand Your Ground —
TO KILL, OR NOT TO KILL...

PROLOGUE
Notions of Self-defense

In the Ed Parker system of "Kenpo Karate"[1], the Kenpo Creed touches upon the notion of self-defense when it proposes that,

> *"...should I be forced to defend myself, my principles or my honor, should it be a matter of life or death, right or wrong, then here are my weapons, 'Karate' – my empty hands."*

Unfortunately for many defendants charged with the unlawful use of force, empty hands are not always

---

[1] These are, reportedly, Japanese words, despite the fact that Kenpo Karate is considered to primarily have its origins in Chinese martial arts. In Japanese, Kenpo means "law of the fist," and Karate means "empty hands." Ed Parker's Kenpo Karate ("EPKK") diverged from Japanese Shotokan Karate in the sense that it no longer sacrificed speed for power and also in its practical "partner" techniques of defending against various choreographed attacks. In the 1970s, EPKK student David Brock later developed the concept of "broken-rhythm" in fighting, which again revolutionized hand-to-hand combat. Instead of charging in for a strike, a fighter would make threatening moves in a rhythm which was unpredictable to his opponent, then actually strike before the opponent could move away, block or parry the blow. Mixed Martial Arts, involving ground techniques of a version of Japanese jujitsu refined by the Gracie family in Brazil, was the next major evolutionary step of weaponless martial arts.

Prologue

the instrument of harm. The Courts are filled with criminal prosecutions and civil lawsuits alleging assault, battery, wrongful death, manslaughter and murder by alleged perpetrators using deadly weapons. But "empty hands" can also convey the unlawful use of deadly force.

For example, in *McKnight v. State* (Fla.App. 3 Dist. 1977) 341 So.2d 261[2], the Court held that the female defendant acted in self-defense where she had no where to run, extracted a gun from her purse and shot her **unarmed** assailant, killing him. In *McKnight*, the victim, a large, strong man who had been living with defendant, beat defendant with his fists to her head, and again at a bar, throwing her against a door. Later at her home, the man threatened to seriously beat her and continued towards defendant after having been warned to stop. The Court, in *McKnight*, held that when the prosecution completed its proof of these facts at trial, defendant was entitled to a directed verdict of acquittal of Manslaughter, since the shooting constituted reasonable force to repel the deadly force of the unarmed attack by the victim. *See also, Cook v. State* (Miss. 1943) 12 So.2d 137, 194 Miss. 467

---

[2] The case citations that you see in this book are legal shorthand for lengthier book titles. In this case, 341 So.2d 261 means volume 341 of Southern Reports, Second Edition, at the starting page of 261. The shorthand version of case citations, including the name of the case, is how cases may be located and read in full on the internet, through on-line legal research systems such as WestLaw or Lexis, or at any well-stocked Law Library.

Stand Your Ground —
TO KILL, OR NOT TO KILL...

(deadly force may be reasonably necessary in self-defense in a fist fight where there is a substantial size differential between the combatants and the force applied by the unarmed attacker is or reasonably appears to be likely to cause death or great bodily injury).

In *Robert v. Boudreaux* (La.App. 5 Cir. 1985) 472 So.2d 166, two male intruders, one of whom was six feet one inch tall, appeared on the female defendant's property under circumstances where, since they blocked defendant's path, there was no possible avenue of retreat. Defendant had information given to her by a neighbor as to the wrongful intentions of the intruders and defendant was unable to summons anyone nearby for help. The Court in *Boudreaux* held that defendant's act in shooting and wounding one of the unarmed intruders when he turned suddenly and moved toward her was justified as self-defense since she had a reasonable fear of imminent harm from force likely to cause death or great bodily injury.

Since there is an obvious and understandable focus in the various martial arts on defense against wrongful injury, it would of course be helpful to martial artists, and to everyone else who has concern for the future, to have a clear understanding of the **legal parameters** of the defense of necessity commonly known as "self-defense."

Prologue

However, despite the fact that I am a criminal defense and civil litigation lawyer by profession (*one* of my professions), this writing is ***not*** intended to comprehensively instruct *lawyers* in the arcane intricacies of national, state and local legal statutes, ordinances and case law pertaining to self-defense. There are ample judicial opinions, statutes, scholarly treatises, digests and encyclopedias focused on affording those in the legal profession an exhaustive and microscopic view of this very broad area of the law.

The present work is intended to inform the **everyday citizen** (including, of course, martial artists) to help prepare him or her[3] to stand ready to make a lawful split-second decision when an attacker is in his midst.[4] The sound judgment of these defenders will tend to save lives, avoid civil and criminal sanctions and preserve honor.

---

[3] For simplicity, all further references to "him and her" or "him or her," and "his and her" or "his or her," are simply made by stating "him" or "his," respectively.

[4] **Important Disclaimer:** This work is not intended to offer legal advice pertaining to any past, present or future conduct and should not be relied upon as a substitute for the reader retaining his own independent counsel for legal advice which is specific to the particular legal jurisdiction in which the reader finds himself when a legal issue arises. Also, the various scenarios set forth herein are fictional and not intended to depict any actual events which have occurred. Any similarity to any actual events or persons referred to herein is unintended and coincidental.

Stand Your Ground —
TO KILL, OR NOT TO KILL...

The Safest Course

General principles of self-defense have a lengthy and colorful history in case law throughout the United States. For example, in an 1875 case, a West Virginia Court held that self-defense, as a defense to a Murder or Manslaughter prosecution, requires proof of both a belief and a reasonable basis for the belief that **at the moment of killing the deceased**, defendant was in imminent danger to his life or of great bodily harm by the unlawful use of force from the deceased. In *Abbott*, defendant was "lying in wait" for the victim. The Court wrote, "Previous threats or acts of hostility, however relevant they may be, will not justify a person in seeking and slaying his adversary." *State v. Abbott* (W.Va. 1875) 8 W.Va. 741. The legal right to kill another person is based on *necessity*, real or apparent. *State v. Cox* (Me. 1941) 23 A.2d 634, 138 Me. 151.

Nevertheless, in **virtually any real-life encounter**, there is an insidious **X-factor** which comes into play. You may think of the X-factor in this sense as being similar to Murphy's Law: **Whatever can go wrong will go wrong**. There are few easy guarantees in life, and this holds particularly true in the system of justice **anywhere** in the world, including in the United States.

---

[5] The author's opinion in this regard is not an endorsement, however, for a State requiring a "duty to retreat" in its laws pertaining to defense against unlawful force. The "stand your ground" laws would appear, for a variety of reasons subsequently discussed in this book, to be the rule providing **the most predictable and sound safeguards** for

Prologue

Even if you find yourself **completely justified** and clearly within your rights to use force against another person, the most **prudent** course may still be to **retreat** to safety rather than engage in a physical battle with the assailant.[5]

When a **completely safe retreat** is, in fact, reasonably available to you, by definition it amounts to a **guaranteed result of safety**. Also, a safe retreat has the key benefit of **avoiding legal controversy** as to any further physical contact with your assailant. Of course, **finding and availing oneself of** the completely safe retreat may prove elusive.

Without an effective retreat, the X-factor may come into play with a **decidedly adverse effect** upon you as the defender, including that:

(1) you may **under**estimate your opponent and lose the battle;

(2) you may **over**estimate your own fighting skills and lose the battle;

(3) other perpetrators may come to your opponent's aid;

---

the defender, while **still adequately protecting the safety of the assailant**. The "stand your ground" States generally do not allow a trier of fact to **second-guess** a defender's conduct by **hypothesizing** about whether a completely safe retreat, of which the defendant was aware, did or did not exist.

Stand Your Ground—
TO KILL, OR NOT TO KILL...

(4) bystanders may misunderstand the situation and may come to your opponent's aid;

(5) there may be *no* other witnesses and later it will become a "liars contest" between you and your opponent;

(6) there may be witnesses who are biased and who will lie to protect your attacker;

(7) there may be witnesses who innocently misperceive or mistakenly recall the events;

(8) by the time a witness testifies at trial, preliminary examination or deposition, the witness may have forgotten key facts;

(9) a police officer's or private investigator's investigation may adversely influence witnesses against you;

(10) a police officer may fail to accurately chronicle the events and witness interviews;

(11) a prosecutor or civil plaintiff's lawyer may have an agenda which is unfair, biased or otherwise prejudicial to your interests;

(12) the risk of going to trial and losing, or the expense of undertaking a proper legal defense, may cause you to compromise (in criminal law, by a "plea bargain").

Prologue

(13) jury members may not understand your particular point of reference in the affray or may even be intellectually or culturally **incapable** of fully understanding your point of reference;

(14) the prosecutor or civil plaintiff's lawyer may be more skilled in advocacy and trial work than your defense lawyer; and

(15) as a result of any combination of the foregoing possibilities you may be wrongfully convicted or wrongfully found civilly liable for your acts of violence.

However, if you *must* respond to an imminent threat or attack with physical force, then is imperative that you have a thorough knowledge of

Stand Your Ground—
TO KILL, OR NOT TO KILL...
The Legal Limits of Safety

Stand Your Ground—
TO KILL, OR NOT TO KILL...

OVERVIEW

"*He may lay his hands upon him softly, and if he then resist, force may be used.*"

McCoy v. State (Ark. 1848) 8 Ark. 451, 3 Eng. 451[6]

Fundamental Right...with Limits

An early California Court of Appeal decision held that the right of a person to repel a violent and wrongful assault by another person is a **law of nature antedating all written enactments.** *People v. Turpin* (1909) 10 Cal.App. 526, 102 P. 680.

Self-defense was shown to have existed in *State v. Grover* (Idaho 1920) 207 P. 1080, 35 Idaho 589 when an accused was attacked by the deceased with a shovel. There, defendant managed to block the first strike with defendant's own shovel, dodged a second strike and fatally struck the deceased when the deceased was in the course of delivering still a third blow.

---

[6] The Court commented as to the level of permissible force in ejecting a person from one's home.

Overview

There are, of course, obvious **limits** to the self-defense doctrine. For example, in *Com. v. Sheppard* (Pa. Super. 1994) 648 A.2d 563, 436 Pa.Super. 584, following verbal arguments, defendant obtained an axe from another room, pursued the deceased and struck him **seventeen times with the axe**! Not surprisingly, the Court held that defendant's belief in the need to defend himself with deadly force was unreasonable and that the defense of self-defense had not been established.

In *State v. Diggs* (Conn. 1991) 592 A.2d 949, 219 Conn. 295, the defendant kept a rifle in his hands trained on a homicide victim and communicated to the victim what amounted to a demand for the victim to withdraw. When the victim did **not** withdraw from the encounter or clearly manifest and intent to do so, defendant shot and killed him. The Court in *Diggs* held that since the victim was not the initial aggressor, defendant's killing of the victim was not legally justified.

Another case involved a husband/defendant who testified at trial that his wife had extracted from a kitchen drawer a large kitchen knife and threatened him with it. On appeal of the husband's conviction of murder, the Court in *State v. Anaya* (Ohio App. 6 Dist. 2010) 947 N.E.2d 212, 191 Ohio App.3d 602 held that even assuming the truth of defendant's testimony, his subsequent conduct of disarming his wife and thereafter **stabbing her with the knife multiple times**,

Stand Your Ground —
TO KILL, OR NOT TO KILL...

killing her, rendered his claim of self-defense untenable and not exculpatory.

In *State v. Crews* (Mo.App.E.D. 1993) 851 S.W.2d 56, no self-defense existed where the defendant took an **axe handle** from the victim, but then hit the victim in the head with it, placed the victim into bed and hit him again with the axe handle. *Crews* held that the result would be the same even if the actual death occurred before defendant's attack in the bedroom, since defendant believed that the victim was still alive in the bedroom and admitted continuing in his attack.

A defendant shot his wife three times after the wife clutched **fingernail clippers**, apparently in a threatening manner. The Court in *State v. Golson* (La.App. 2 Cir. 1995) 658 So.2d 225 held that the attempted murder of the wife by her **250 pound**, **six feet two inch** husband/defendant could not be justified by a claim of self-defense.

Clearly then, **excessive force can negate** an otherwise lawful exercise of self-defense. *Johnson v. United States* (D.C. 2008) 960 A.2d 281. In *Gray v. State* (Md.App. 1968) 241 A.2d 909, 4 Md.App. 175, the deceased was the initial aggressor. However, after defendant shot the deceased once, the deceased fled down deceased's cellar stairs, but was pursued by defendant who **shot him four more times in the back**, killing him. *Gray* held that even while deceased was the initial aggressor, the force exerted by defendant was unreasonable and excessive and self-defense as a

Overview

legal defense in a criminal prosecution was simply not available to the defendant.

Criminal and Civil Law Aspects

In California, the basic notion of the right of self-defense is set forth in California Civil Code Section 50, which reads:

> "Any necessary force may be used to protect from wrongful injury the person or property of oneself, or of a wife, husband, child, parent, or other relative, or member of one's family, or of a ward, servant, master, or guest." (Enacted 1872. Amended by Code Am. 1873-74, c. 612, p. 184, Sect. 12.)

The simplicity of Civil Code Section 50, however, belies the **exceptional complexity** of the law pertaining to the legal parameters of self-defense. In the face of this complexity, some would be inclined to over-simplify the question by reciting the common adage,

> *"Better to be tried by twelve than buried by six."*

While this saying is humorous and even catchy, it can lead to **disastrous unintended results** and is definitely **not** a valid substitute for a person's studied understanding of the law pertaining to defending oneself (or loved ones), one's principles, one's honor, or even one's property.

Stand Your Ground —
TO KILL, OR NOT TO KILL...

The legal concept of self-defense typically comes into play when someone is either subject to arrest or prosecution for assault and battery or a homicide, or when someone is sued in a civil lawsuit for damages due to an assault and battery or a homicide. Thus, there are both **criminal law** components and **civil law** components of the legal concept of self-defense. Both the criminal and civil components are grounded in the general idea that every person has the inherent, inalienable right, born out of legal "necessity," to defend themselves or others from an unlawful ("wrongful") attack. Tort rules and criminal law rules regarding self-defense law are virtually identical. *Juarez-Martinez v. Deans* (N.C.App. 1993) 424 S.E.2d 154, 108 N.C.App. 486. However, that having been noted, the laws in these regards may vary from State to State.

New York law specifically **bars** a plaintiff from prosecuting a negligence action once intentional offensive contact has been established. *LaLonde v. Bates* (N.D.N.Y. 2001) 166 F.Supp.2d 713. In Virginia, however, a bar patron's civil action against a security guard and his employer was held to not be barred by the plaintiff's conviction for assault, where plaintiff alleged that the security guard's use of deadly force against plaintiff was excessive. *Godbolt v. Brawley* (Va. 1995) 463 S.E.2d 657, 250 Va. 467.

In *Duprey v. Maryland Management Corp.* (N.Y.A.D. 1954) 127 N.Y.Supp.2d 615, 283 App. Div. 701 a defendant was sued civilly by a plaintiff

Overview

aggressor for personal injuries resulting from the use of excessive force against an unlawful attack. The *Duprey* Court held that the defendant may not be held liable to plaintiff unless defendant's use of excessive force was accompanied by a **specific intent to inflict unnecessary injury** on the plaintiff (i.e., an allegation of mere negligence is insufficient).

The Court, in *Bonpua v. Fagan* (N.J.Super.A.D. 1992) 602 A.2d 287, 253 N.J.Super. 475, considered whether an initial aggressor could **defend** on the grounds of a plaintiff's "comparative fault." In *Bonpua*, the defendant alleged in his defense of a civil action for damages that plaintiff had humiliated him by calling defendant a 'fagot," that plaintiff had exited his vehicle and commenced hitting defendant, and that plaintiff's injuries resulted from defendant simply defending himself. The Court held that defendant's criminal conviction for aggravated assault was not necessarily inconsistent with a finding that his "victim" was civilly responsible in part for his own injuries under a civil comparative fault doctrine. The factual allegations as to plaintiff's provocation of the attack, the Court ruled, were sufficient to state a comparative negligence affirmative defense.

In criminal law, self-defense is considered to be a justification and not an affirmative defense, while civilly, self-defense is pleaded and proved as an affirmative defense. *Gibbons v. Berlin* (Tex.App.—Fort Worth 2005) 162 S.W.3d 335. In a civil case, "[s]elf-defense

Stand Your Ground —
TO KILL, OR NOT TO KILL...

being an affirmative defense, it must be established by the defendant, if at all, by a preponderance of the evidence." *Bartosh v. Banning* (1967) 251 Cal. App.2d 378, 386, 59 Cal.Rptr. 382. While in a criminal prosecution, once the defendant produces evidence constituting a "prima facie" case of self-defense or defense of others, the prosecution in a battery case must rebut this defense by proof **beyond a reasonable doubt** that the defendant's actions were not taken in justifiable defense. *K.S.H. v. State* (Fla. Dist. Ct. App. 3d Dist. 2011) 56 So.3d 122. Where sufficient evidence exists to give rise to a reasonable inference of self-defense, the prosecution must prove the **absence** of self-defense beyond a reasonable doubt. Thus, in a criminal prosecution, the lack of the use of force in lawful self-defense becomes an **element of the crime**, not an affirmative defense. *State v. Olander* (N.D. 1998) 575 N.W.2d 658. In *State v. George* (Wash. 2011) 249 P.3d 202, a murder conviction was overturned where trial court unlawfully thwarted the defendant's attempt to present a defense of self-defense. There, defendant presented ample evidence to suggest that self-defense may be a viable defense and it was then up to a properly instructed jury, not the trial court judge, to determine whether the prosecution had disproved this defense beyond a reasonable doubt.

Self-defense is consistent only with intentional conduct, however, since the perpetrator must subjectively believe that the force was reasonably necessary to protect against imminent harm.

Overview

Accordingly, where a defendant consistently testified that the fatal blow was "accidental," the defense of self-defense was held to be **inapplicable** and unavailable. *State v. Hendrickson* (Wash. App. Div. 1 1996) 914 P.2d 1194, 81 Wash.App. 397. However, if the deceased is accidentally killed in a struggle as a result of falling and striking an object or being struck by an overturned object or the accidental discharge of a weapon during a struggle for its possession, an accused is nevertheless entitled to an acquittal if acting in lawful self-defense. *Bolyard v. Com.* (Va. App. 1990) 397 S.E.2d 894, 11 Va.App. 274.

Individual States in the United States have **statutes** codifying the right of self-defense. For example, Florida Statutes ("Fla. Stat.") 776.012 provides:

> "A person is justified in using force, except deadly force, against another when and to the extent that the person reasonably believes that such conduct is necessary to defend himself or herself or another against the other's imminent use of unlawful force. However, a person is justified in the use of deadly force and **does not have a duty to retreat** if: (1) He or she reasonably believes that such force is necessary to prevent imminent death or great bodily harm to himself or herself or another or to prevent the imminent commission of a forcible felony;

Stand Your Ground —
TO KILL, OR NOT TO KILL...

or (2) Under those circumstances permitted pursuant to 776.013."[7] (bold added for emphasis)

Such lawful use of force in self-defense or in the defense of others renders a person "immune" from criminal conviction and civil liability based upon the use of such force. Fla. Stat. Sect. 776.032(1).

Duty to Retreat

Unlike Florida law, in New York a defendant generally has an **affirmative duty to retreat** and thus is not justified in using deadly force if he realizes that he is **able to retreat with complete safety** as to himself and others. *Davis v. Strack* (2d Cir. 2001) 270 F.3d 111. For example, where a defendant returned to the scene of a prior assault with a baseball bat and knife and thereafter stabbed his attacker, the defense of self-defense was not established since defendant could have retreated from the scene with complete safety. (Here, there would also be lacking the element of imminent harm as we shall see, *infra*). Based on these facts, the defendant's conviction for the stabbing death of the victim was upheld on appeal. *People v. Reyes* (N.Y.A.D. 2 Dept. 1986) 497 N.Y.S.2d 463, 116 A.D.2d 602. If a duty to retreat applies and the State establishes beyond a reasonable doubt that a completely safe retreat was available to the defendant and that defendant was aware of the safe retreat but

---

[7] Fla. Stat. Section 776.013 is discussed in detail later.

Overview

chose to not avail himself thereof, then the elements of the defense of self-defense **cannot** be satisfied. *State v. Saunders* (Conn. 2004) 838 A.2d 186, 267 Conn. 363.

However, even where a duty to retreat is part of the State's defense-justification law, there is no duty to retreat **where retreat is not feasible**. An inmate/defendant, assaulted by his cellmate, was held to have had no duty to retreat prior to using deadly force to kill his assailant, where the Court pointed out that the homicide occurred in the defendant's cell, defendant was obligated by law to occupy that cell, the cell was 7½ feet by 10 feet and retreat was never an option. *State v. Cassano* (Ohio 2002) 772 N.E.2d 81, 96 Ohio St.3d 94.

An excellent example of the **perverse results** that can result from an unbridled **duty to retreat** law is the case of *State v. Kennamore* (Tenn. 1980) 604 S.W.2d 856[8]. There, the defendant and another person accompanied the deceased to a secluded area along a country road, where they built a campfire for an evening of drinking beer and socializing. At some propitious moment in the evening, while defendant was kneeling to tend the fire, the deceased **struck defendant viciously** on

---

[8] The "duty to retreat" legal framework embodied in *Kennamore* was effectively superceded by *State v. Renner* (Tenn. 1995) 912 S.W.2d 701 which acknowledged that Tennessee had since joined the majority of jurisdictions in the United States by codifying the "no duty to retreat" "true man" doctrine of self-defense. (912 S.W.2d at 703-704)

Stand Your Ground —
TO KILL, OR NOT TO KILL...

the head from behind with a beer bottle. Severely injured, defendant reached his shotgun and fired, killing the deceased with a lone blast. At trial, defendant in *Kennamore* was convicted of Voluntary Manslaughter. On appeal, the Tennessee Court of Criminal Appeals **affirmed** the conviction! *Kennamore* held that the trial Judge **correctly refused** to instruct the jury on the "True Man" defense wherein the victim of an unprovoked attack that threatens death or serious bodily injury has no duty to retreat prior to responding with deadly force. The Court ruled that the "True Man" defense **is limited to the defense of home or habitation**. Apparently the underlying rationale of the ruling is that having been struck to the back of the head forcefully with a beer bottle, in a secluded area with no assurance of any assistance, and with the defendant having been severely injured by the beer bottle assault, the defendant **failed to exhaust his obligation to retreat** prior to being further assaulted with deadly force by the deceased and prior to the defendant responding with deadly force. This is a 1980 case that sounds more like a 1780 case.

In *People v. Aiken* (N.Y. 2005) 828 N.E.2d 74, 795 N.Y.Supp.2d 158, 4 N.Y.3d 324, defendant had been stabbed in the back by the victim, who confronted defendant at defendant's doorway in a multi-unit apartment building. The victim reached into his pocket, came up to defendant's face, nose-to-nose, and announced that he was going to kill defendant. The *Aiken* Court acknowledged the principles of an

Overview

exception to the duty to retreat which is generally known as the "**Castle Doctrine**," stating that,

> "...[O]ne should not be driven from the inviolate place of refuge that is the home. 'It is not now, and never has been the law that a man assailed in his own dwelling, is bound to retreat. If assailed there, he may stand his ground, and resist the attack. **He is under no duty to take to the fields and the highways, a fugitive from his own home**' (see *People v. Tomlins*, 213 N.Y. 240, 243, 107 N.E. 496 [1914, Cardozo, J.])." (*Aiken, supra*, 795 N.Y.Supp.2d at 161, bold added for emphasis)

However, *Aiken* pointed out that the general rule in New York law was that a defender has **a duty to retreat** prior to resort to deadly force to repel an attack. The Court explained that,

> "'The duty to retreat reflects the idea that a killing is justified only as a last resort, an act impermissible as long as other reasonable avenues are open.' ...Indeed, requiring a defender to retreat before using deadly force may in fact be the 'more civilized view'..." (*Aiken, supra*, 795 N.Y.Supp.2d at 161)

Applying the duty to retreat rule, the Court, in *Aiken, affirmed* defendant's murder conviction, reasoning that before defendant was entitled to defend himself using deadly force, he must **first retreat into his apartment**,

Stand Your Ground—
TO KILL, OR NOT TO KILL...

"Here, defendant need only have closed the door, or pulled up the drawbridge, to be secure in his castle." (795 N.Y.Supp.2d at 163)

On **virtually indistinguishable facts** and also in a "duty to retreat" State, the Court in *State v. Bonano* (NJ 1971) 284 A.2d 345, 59 N.J. 515 held that the defendant could **stand his ground** and defend himself even with the use of deadly force. There, defendant had been **standing in his own doorway** when the victim approached and mounted the steps, drew his knife and threatened to kill the defendant. *Bonano* reiterated that,

"...'When it comes to a question whether one man shall flee or another man shall live, the law decides that the former shall rather flee than that the latter shall die.' *Commonwealth v. Drum*, 58 Pa.St. 9, 22 (1868)." (59 N.J. at 519)

However, perhaps recognizing the **unjust result** of requiring defendant in these facts to lose the right of self-defense, the Court, in *Bonano*, **construed** that **defendant was, in fact, "inside" his home when he was in the doorway**, since a "porch or other similar physical appurtenance" is **deemed** to fall within the exception to the duty to retreat when an assailant enters the dwelling house (59 N.J. at 520). *Bonano* held that the trial court's **failure** to instruct the jury that defendant had **no legal duty to withdraw indoors** was reversible prejudicial error.

Overview

Common-sense and the Right to Defense

To understand issues of the legal parameters of the right to physical safety defense, the following questions might be asked:

1. What constitutes an unlawful attack?

2. What is the effect of mutually consented-to combat upon the defense of self-defense?

3. May the defender stand his ground or is there a duty to retreat in the particular State in which the defender finds himself at the time of the use of force?

4. What are the **limits of force** implicit in the concept of the right of self-defense to an unlawful attack?

5. How does a person **lose** the right of self-defense?

6. What are the practical ramifications of the right of self-defense in a civil lawsuit versus in a criminal prosecution?

7. How is the **use** of a weapon treated differently from **no** use of weapon in the law of self-defense?

8. What are the risks of one's conduct being misunderstood or misinterpreted by witnesses, police, prosecutors, a Judge or jury? And,

Stand Your Ground —
TO KILL, OR NOT TO KILL...

9. How can the average person decide, in the critical moments before an attack and in view of the varying rules of law from State to State, whether and to what extent they may be entitled to use force upon another person?

Instead of viewing these and other pertinent questions in the abstract, however, the pertinent legal principles can be best understood by examining a series of **Scenarios** in which various fact patterns raise corresponding legal issues. Using these scenarios, applicable, sometimes competing, legal principles will be cited and the facts will be applied to the law. Lawyers might recognize this approach as being similar to a series of Bar Exam essay questions[9]. The difference is that here, the "exam questions" will all pertain to physical violence and to the defense of necessity. Also, unlike in the Bar Exam, I will be writing the answers for you!

---

[9] The California Bar Exam was, and is, a very strenuous, multiple-day examination of every subject a law student typically learns over a three-year, full-time, course of study in law school. There are essay questions and multiple choice questions. The first-time pass rate in California is typically below 50% — i.e., more than half of the people taking the test for the first time fail. I happened to beat the odds and passed the first time I took the exam since I was one of those students who took law school very seriously and put everything into my studies. As a memento of the testing, I still have the original test question booklets handed out for that Bar Exam date many years ago.

Scenario One
Basic Self-defense

Facts: A is shopping at a grocery store at 11:00 a.m. and is spun around by a young and physically capable man, B, who begins to hit him in his face and body. A defends himself against this attack by knocking B unconscious by an inward elbow strike to B's head. A promptly calls 9-1-1 and when the police arrive, A is arrested and charged with battery.

Analysis: It is widely recognized and black-letter law (i.e., so universally established that it is beyond reasonable dispute) that society owes to its citizens the right of self-defense, such that generally, a person who is attacked unlawfully, or with unreasonable force, should be entitled to take reasonable measures to defend himself from physical harm. In that circumstance, the defender's intentional acts of inflicting harm upon an attacker are considered to be legally justified and a complete "defense," such that he is not guilty of any crime (nor responsible in monetary damages for civil battery) arising from the use of such physical force. In Scenario One, there is no proper

Stand Your Ground —
TO KILL, OR NOT TO KILL...

justification for B's unprovoked attack on A, and thus, B's attack is clearly "unlawful." According to the undisputed facts, B is "physically capable" and pummels A to the face and body. The attack consists, apparently, of strikes by B with his fists which are generally[10] considered to not constitute "deadly force." The law is clear in stating that so long as (1) A actually believes that he needs to defend himself, and (2) a reasonable person in A's position would believe that A needed to defend himself against imminent harm, then (3) A may use reasonable non-deadly force in the degree and manner as is reasonably necessary to defend himself.

In this case, A was hit unexpectedly to the face and body by B. Under these circumstances, it could be **presumed** that A actually believed that he needed to defend himself. As a practical matter, if A testified, it would be expected that A would describe his actual belief that he needed to use force to protect himself.

---

[10] As we have seen above, however, **it is not necessarily the *means* of applying the force *but the force itself*** which determines whether an attack is considered "deadly". It is clear that the blunt-force trauma from even a single fist, elbow, knee or foot to the unlucky recipient can result in death. Also, a series of unarmed strikes against a person may be likely to result in death or great bodily injury, particularly where the victim is at a physical disadvantage or is rendered increasingly helpless by the assailant's attack. For purposes of the instant Scenario, however, the weaponless attack will be considered to be an application of **non-deadly** force.

Scenario One

Moreover, a reasonable person in A's position would also likely believe that he needed to defend himself against imminent harm, considering the volley of unprovoked blows and the fact that B was a physically capable man. Finally, the level of force used by A—an inward-elbow strike to B's temple—was non-deadly, merely rendering B unconscious, and was reasonable in both manner and degree of force. The fact that he is skilled in the fighting arts will not be used as a basis for denying A the right to use reasonable force, and simply knocking someone unconscious without more is not "deadly force" in the legal sense as will be explained later in this book. Moreover, considering the fact that the violence against A was sudden and unexpected, there would be no completely safe retreat that could be attained, even if this fight took place in a "duty to retreat" State. Finally, calling the police was the right thing to do, and any prosecution of A for battery should fail because the elements for a claim of self-defense have been met. In a criminal prosecution where a trial Judge finds that the undisputed material facts establish a valid defense of self-defense, a motion to dismiss by the defendant should be granted. *State v. Smith* (Fla. Dist. Ct. App. 3d Dist. 1979) 376 So.2d 261.

Stand Your Ground—
TO KILL, OR NOT TO KILL...

Scenario Two
Fear of Assault or Battery Not Rising to the Level of Bodily Harm

Facts: On a cold night, A, a 6 foot tall, 200 pound man in his 50s in good physical shape, is standing in a somewhat uneven line to purchase a movie ticket when a younger man, B, of similar physical stature from immediately behind A accuses him of, "Hey, excuse me but you **cut the line**." A informs B, "I didn't cut any line. I've been standing here the whole time," but B is loudly insistent that A "cut the line!" With his index finger of his right hand, B proceeds to poke A in the chest repeatedly, telling A to, "Move it, buddy, get outta line. **Move** it!" A warns B to stop poking him but B persists and in retaliation, A shoves B with moderate force. B trips over a small child standing behind him, strikes his head on the concrete and suffers serious traumatic brain injury. The child was not injured. Theater personnel summon the police and A is placed under arrest for aggravated battery. When A is arrested, he admits to police that he did not fear imminent

Scenario Two

bodily harm from B, but states that the poking in his chest was annoying. A further states to police that he didn't feel like he had to just stand there and take it. A states that he never intended for B to fall down or to hit his head on the concrete. Other witnesses confirm that A did not cut into the line and that B was mistaken in that belief. The movie theatre exterior video camera also confirms that A did not cut into the line.

Analysis: No words or gestures by the victim, however abusive or insulting, if not otherwise constituting a threat of imminent harm, will justify as self-defense the use of force upon the verbally abusive person. *Jones People v. Lopez. State* (1892) 96 Ala. 102, 11 So. 399; *Crosby v. People* (1891) 137 Ill. 325, 27 N.E. 49; *State v. Frommett* (1968 Iowa) 159 N.W.3d 532; *Harper v. Commonwealth* (1955) 196 Va. 723, 85 S.E.2d 249. Mere insults, alone as opposed to threats are, as a matter of law, not sufficient to justify self-defense. *People v. Gordon* (N.Y.D.D. 1 Dept. 1996) 636 N.Y.S.2d 317, 223 A.2d 372. Vile epithets were no justification for killing the deceased in response. *Adams v. Com.* (Va. 1935) 178 S.E. 29, 163 Va. 1053.

The Vermont Supreme Court, in *Willey v. Carpenter* (Vt. 1892) 23 A. 630, 64 Vt. 212, aptly articulated this **time-honored** rule of law:

"The alleged speeches and conduct of the plaintiff, although for the purpose of provoking

Stand Your Ground —
TO KILL, OR NOT TO KILL...

the defendant to strike him, are no defense. Mere words, however gross and abusive, cannot justify an assault and battery...The acts of the plaintiff in 'malignantly' leering at the defendant and in making taunting grimaces at him were provocations of the same character as insulting and provoking language. None of these acts were of such a character as to amount to an assault by the plaintiff upon the defendant; and in order to justify him in striking in self-defense, the act complained of must constitute an assault." (23 A. at 631)

When insulting or contemptuous epithets **actually result in combat**, the one speaking them and inciting the conflict **may not claim self-defense** in defending against the ensuing attack. *Scott v. Com.* (Va. 1925) 129 S.E. 360, 143 Va. 510. *See also to this effect: Hays v. Territory* (Okla. Terr. 1897) 52 P. 950 (gross insult and obloquy); *State v. Strickland* (S.C.App. 2010) 697 S.E.2d 681, 389 S.C. 210 (opprobrious language likely to result in a physical attack).

However, in the instant scenario, B's conduct of accusing and insulting A (calling him, in effect, a cheating line-cutter) went beyond words and gestures, and quickly escalated into **repeated pokes** to A's chest, accompanied by **taunting commands** to A to "move it." Although these facts border on creating a reasonable belief in imminent physical harm, in this case A admits to police that he had no actual (i.e.,

Scenario Two

subjective) belief that B was about to physically harm him. A did, however, subjectively want the offensive chest poking to stop and expressly told B to stop it. B persisted and A retaliated physically by pushing the man away with moderate force.

A's retaliation under these circumstances of shoving B away from himself was lawful self-defense. A person may lawfully defend himself from bodily injury **or offensive physical touching** *even where he is not threatened with death or great bodily injury*. *Juarez-Martinez v. Deans* (N.C.App. 1993) 424 S.E.2d 154, 108 N.C.App. 486.

In *People v. Myers* (1998) 61 Cal.App.4th 328, 71 Cal.Rptr. 518, a defendant was charged with aggravated assault and battery over an incident where he had been **poked in the chest** by a man with whom he had had previous arguments. Defendant responded by pushing the man, who slipped on the wet pavement, struck his head and suffered serious head injuries. Claiming self-defense, defendant requested that the trial court give a jury instruction on self-defense but this defense request was **denied**. Defendant was convicted of the charges and appealed. On appeal, the California Court of Appeal held that **the trial court was in error** in refusing to give the requested instruction on self-defense to a jury. The Court reasoned that **a person may resist a simple battery, regardless of the lack of a threat of imminent bodily injury,** and that,

Stand Your Ground —
TO KILL, OR NOT TO KILL...

"To hold otherwise would lead to the ludicrous result of a person not being able to lawfully resist or defend against a continuing assault or battery." (61 Cal.App.4th at 335)

In our scenario, then, A's shoving of B in retaliation for the finger poking would be considered legally justified under the defense of self-defense. The fact that B tripped over a child and received severe head injuries as an unintended result would not be determinative of the underlying self-defense issues. Moreover, the fact of whether A did or did not cut in line is a red-herring, and would not affect the result either way. If A had cut in line, the proper resolution would have been to ask him to go to the back of the line, to contact movie personnel or to ignore it and enjoy the movie; not to make a scene and poke the offender repeatedly in the chest. Any prosecution of A for battery would fail and A would bear no civil liability to anyone for B's serious brain injuries.

Scenario Three
Deadly Force and the Defense of Others

Facts: A, a physically fit ex-college baseball pitcher in his 40s is shopping in a grocery store at 11:00 a.m. and notices a **heated verbal argument** between B and C, in a corner of the store. B and C are both in their mid-20s and of similar size and stature. A observes B to hit C in the face and C to extract a **combat knife** from his front pocket. B backs up and C waves the knife in a threatening manner and tells B, "You're a dead man now." Then, C begins to move in to cut B as B is trapped between the fresh vegetable counter and the arranged flowers. Fearing for B's life, A grabs a **can of peas** and hurls it as hard as he can directly at C's head, striking C in the temple. C is killed instantly from the flying can of peas trauma. Police arrive on the scene and arrest A for Voluntary Manslaughter.

Analysis: The right to defend others from unlawful attack is a **legal corollary** to the right of self-defense, and in most jurisdictions, this doctrine states

Stand Your Ground—
TO KILL, OR NOT TO KILL...

generally that a person may act in a manner which he subjectively and reasonably believes is reasonably necessary in order to repel an unlawful attack against another person. In California, Penal Code Sections 692 through 694 set forth the statutory laws which permit a person to undertake "resistance sufficient to prevent" an offense against a family member or other person "about to be injured." For example, in *People v. McKee* (1968) 265 Cal.App.2d 53, 61, 71 Cal.Rptr. 26, a California Court of Appeal held that a defendant bar owner who came to the aid of a woman patron harassed by other patrons was entitled to a jury instruction on the legal defense of defense of others.

However, throughout the United States, the law has traditionally[11] distinguished between the lawfulness of the use, in self-defense, of **"deadly force"** versus **"non-deadly force."** Generally, deadly force is defined as force likely to cause death or great bodily injury. In California, Penal Code Section 198.5 defines the term "great bodily injury" as being **a significant**

---

[11] In many jurisdictions within the United States, the concept of deadly versus non-deadly force is becoming **superseded** by legal principles which simply allow **any degree of force which is reasonably necessary** to repel the force applied. In California, for example, the Jury instruction for self-defense commonly utilized in criminal prosecutions for Battery and Murder states in pertinent part, "...In the exercise of his right of self-defense a person may stand his ground and defend himself by the use of **all force and means which would appear to be necessary** to a reasonable person in a similar situation and with similar knowledge..." CALJIC 5.50 Self-Defense (bold added for emphasis).

Scenario Three

or substantial physical injury. In *Shorter v. People* (1849) 2 N.Y. 193, 51 Am. Dec. 286, the Supreme Court of New York held that one may justifiably kill his adversary in self-defense (i.e., use deadly force) if he reasonably believes that the adversary has, "a design to take away his life, or to do him some great bodily harm" and that the danger is imminent in the sense that such design will be accomplished if self-defense is not undertaken.

On the other hand, the mere **threat** of deadly force, such as the **brandishing** of a knife, may not qualify as the use of deadly force. For example, in *People v. Wong* (1947) 83 Cal.App.2d 60, 187 P.2d 828, the Court of Appeals held that a claim of self-defense was not available where a defendant twice shot a victim whose only hostile gesture was to take a few steps in defendant's direction. Moreover, injuries as may commonly be associated with **fist fights** do not constitute great bodily injury for purposes of the defense of self-defense. *State v. Doherty* (Or. 1908) 98 P. 152, 52 Or. 591.

However, in the heat of the moment, in the face of imminent danger, a person will not be expected to perfectly gauge or otherwise minimize the degree of force necessary to repel an attack, and **the force used in response will not be considered unlawful unless clearly excessive.** *Silas v. Bowen* (1967, DC SC) 277 F.Supp. 314; *State v. Perkins* (1914) 88 Conn. 360, 91 A. 265; *People v. Pearl* (1889) 76 Mich. 207, 42 N.W.

Stand Your Ground —
TO KILL, OR NOT TO KILL...

1109; *State v. Miller* (1958) 253 Minn. 112, 91 N.W.2d 138; and *State v. Hickam* (1888) 95 Mo. 322, 8 S.W. 252. "Detached reflection" is not required of someone defending against a dangerous or deadly attack. *Dupre v. Maryland Management Corp.* (N.Y.A.D. 1954) 127 N.Y.Supp.2d 615, 283 App.Div. 701.

In the present Scenario, A uses force to defend another person, B, from attack. Although B seems to have started the combat with C by hitting C in the face, C retaliates by pulling a combat knife, waving it at B and threatening B by telling him, "You're a dead man now." In *State v. Lucero* (2010) 147 N.M. 747, 228 P.3d 1167, the New Mexico Supreme Court held that a single "punch in the face" is not a sufficient threat to justify the use of deadly force in response, since it is,

> "not the type of force that creates a high probability of death, results in serious disfigurement, results in loss of any member or organ of the body or results in the permanent prolonged impairment of the use of any member or organ of the body."

When B punches C in the face, it is **highly doubtful** that C would be legally justified to respond by attacking B with (the deadly force of) a combat knife. Although a mere threat of using a knife may not justify fear of imminent deadly force, C's conduct of waving the knife and verbally threatening B's life in relatively close quarters goes well beyond a mere brandishing

Scenario Three

of a weapon. Moreover, C removes all doubt as to his intentions when he actually moves "in to cut B." Accordingly, in this manner, C very likely **loses** the right of self-defense to B's attack since C's **response to B's non-deadly force attack was unreasonable in degree of force.**

Meanwhile, A is a physically fit athlete who happens to be an expert in pitching baseballs. When he picks up the can of peas and prepares to hurl it at C's head, the force which he intends to create is likely to cause death or great bodily injury if it strikes its intended target. Hence, the flying can of peas becomes a deadly weapon under the circumstances. A reasonable person in A's position would be justified, however, in using deadly force to repel C's knife attack on B. This is true since C's attack of B with the combat knife constitutes the wrongful use of deadly force. Accordingly, the corresponding use of deadly force by A to stop C is inherently reasonable, justified and would be a complete defense to the Voluntary Manslaughter[12] prosecution.

---

[12] In California, Manslaughter is generally the killing of another human being without malice. It is of three kinds: (a) Voluntary Manslaughter—upon a sudden quarrel or heat of passion. (b) Involuntary Manslaughter—in the commission of an unlawful act, not amounting to a felony; or in the commission of a lawful act which might produce death, in an unlawful manner, or without due caution and circumspection. And, (c) Vehicular... (California Penal Code Section 192).

Stand Your Ground—
TO KILL, OR NOT TO KILL...

Scenario Four
Actual Harm Versus Perceived Harm

Facts: A petite woman in her 50s is walking alone at 9:00 p.m. in a lighted parking lot after work. The Parking Attendant has already left for the day. B, a casually dressed man in his 30s wearing dirt-stained pants and sweatshirt approaches and asks her for $5.00. A spots two other men, apparently friends of B, standing about 25 yards away, watching. **Previously, A has been assaulted and robbed twice in the same parking lot by homeless men**. As A unlocks her car door, B walks within ten feet behind her, again asking to "borrow five bucks for gas." A pulls a rattan fighting stick from her front seat, turns and violently hits the approaching B once to the head, killing him instantly. She calls 9-1-1. When police arrive, they determine that B had no weapon and no criminal record. He was a cook at a restaurant by profession. Speaking to the two friends of B who had been watching this unfold, police determine that they had all played in a pickup softball game that night and that B was dirty from sliding into home

Scenario Four

plate. The police checked their car and it had, indeed, run out of gas and none of the men had any cash or credit cards to purchase fuel for the return drive home. The friends confirmed to police that B had approached A to ask for a loan of $5.00 so that they could get back to their town, 20 miles away. A is arrested and charged with murder.

Analysis: Regarding self-defense, *actual* danger is not the pertinent issue; a **reasonable belief** of imminent danger is the pertinent issue. As stated clearly in the California jury instruction pertaining to a criminal prosecution,

> "Actual danger is not necessary to justify self-defense. If one is confronted by the appearance of danger which arouses in his mind, as a reasonable person, an actual belief and fear that he is about to suffer bodily injury, and if a reasonable person in a like situation, seeing and knowing the same facts, would be justified in believing himself in like danger, and if that individual so confronted acts in self-defense upon these appearances and from that fear and actual beliefs, the person's right of self-defense is the same whether the danger is real or merely apparent." CALJIC 5.51 Self-Defense—Actual Danger Not Necessary.

In *Vaughn v. Jonas* (1948) 31 Cal.2d 586, 191 P.2d 432, the California Supreme Court held that,

Stand Your Ground —
TO KILL, OR NOT TO KILL...

> "The right of self-defense is not limited by actualities. The correct rule...[is]: 'Generally..., the force that one may use in self-defense is that which reasonably appears necessary, in view of all the circumstances of the case, to prevent the impending injury.' In emphasizing that the law of self-defense is a law of necessity, courts should never lose sight of the fact that the necessity may be either real or apparent." (31 Cal.2d at 599-600)

In *People v. Dawson* (1948) 88 Cal.App.2d 85, 198 P.2d 338, the Court held that a defendant is entitled to act on an honest and reasonable belief that imminent danger exists, and that apparent necessity is enough:

> "If defendant acted from reasonable and honest convictions, he cannot be held criminally responsible for a mistake in the actual extent of the danger, when other reasonable men would alike have been mistaken." (88 Cal.App.2d at 96)

Actual imminent danger is not required in order to make a claim of self-defense. It is sufficient that the defendant reasonably believed that he was at risk of imminent harm. *State v. Douglas* (Wash.App. Div. 2 2005) 116 P.3d 1012, 128 Wash.App. 555. Where defendant and the deceased had exchanged peaceable words of disagreement but the deceased thereafter approached defendant with his **hand on his pistol pocket** as if ready to draw and fire, defendant was

Scenario Four

lawfully justified in firing first, despite the fact that it was **later** determined that the deceased had had no weapon. *DeArman v. State* (Ala. 1882) 71 Ala. 351.

As noted in *State of Marr* (2001) 362 Md. 467, 765 A.2d 645, an honest and objectively reasonable belief may, for a plethora of reasons, turn out to be mistaken, but this does not strip the person of the right to exercise self-defense:

> "The perception that serves as the impetus for responsive action may be incorrect for a variety of reasons, ranging from ignorance of relevant facts that, if known, would put the situation in a different light, to distortions in sensory perceptions, to judgmental errors in the instantaneous assimilation and appreciation of the apparent situation."

The legal principle of a "reasonable person" is that of a hypothetical person of ordinary mental and physical capacity who is as prudent and careful as any situation would require him to be. *People v. Jefferson* (2004) 119 Cal.App.4th 508, 14 Cal.Rptr.3d 473. There are vital public policy reasons for requiring that a defendant's subjective belief of imminent danger be **objectively reasonable**. Without a reference point of a reasonably prudent person, a defendant's subjective beliefs could conveniently justify virtually **every** homicide. *State v. Janes* (1993) 850 P.2d 495, 121 Wash.2d 220, 237. The *Janes* Court explained,

> "Applying a purely subjective

Stand Your Ground —
TO KILL, OR NOT TO KILL...

standard in all cases would give free rein to the short-tempered, the pugnacious, and the foolhardy who see threats of harm where the rest of us would not...." [121 Wash.2d at 240; quoting Susan Estrich, *Defending Women*, 88 Mich. L.Rev. 1430, 1435 (1990)].

Whether defensive force is lawful is determined by an objective standard as applied to the circumstances as they appeared **to the person acting in self-defense** at the time of the altercation. *Shreiteh v. State* (Fla. Dist. Ct. App. 4th Dist. 2008) 987 So.2d 761. In *State v. Hill* (1969) 458 P.2d 171, 76 Wash.2d 557, 566, the Washington Supreme Court explicated further that if defendant were the sole judge of the existence of the danger confronting him and the level and means of force necessary to protect himself against it, "there would be no limit to the amount of force which a person could use in defending himself against such alleged peril." The objective aspect of the standard, **"keeps self-defense firmly rooted in the narrow concept of necessity."** *Janes, supra,* 121 Wash.2d at 240; (bold added for emphasis)

Under the facts as presented in this scenario, A's perception of events is very likely false. B and his friends **actually** needed a loan of gas money to get home and were not on the verge of panhandling from or robbing A. However, equally clear from the facts is that A **actually believed** that B, and his friends as back-

Scenario Four

up if necessary to the attack and robbery, intended to imminently assault and rob A. Considering that A is charged with murder, one question becomes: **Was A's actual, *subjective*, perception of an imminent threat of harm, *objectively reasonable*?** Another way of putting it is whether a reasonable person in A's position would have believed that B's conduct, and the presence of B's friends in close proximity, presented an imminent threat of harm sufficient to justify the use of deadly force in self-defense.

These kinds of **factual issues** are normally the province of a Judge (in a "Court trial" [without a jury]) or Jury (in a "Jury trial" [with a jury]). [*People v. Ranson* (1953) 119 Cal.App.2d 380, 259 P.2d 910; *People v. Bobo* (1960) 184 Cal.App.2d 285, 7 Cal.Rptr. 466], unless the case is on appeal, in which case the appellate court may review whether the evidence was substantial enough, when construed in favor of the party prevailing at trial, to support the verdict.

In the present case, B may reasonably have been mistaken for a homeless man, considering that his clothing was dirty (albeit, from the softball game and sliding into home plate) and considering that he appeared to be panhandling money from A. The Parking Attendant was not present, and there is no indication that any other persons were present in the lot except for B's associates standing off to the side watching. A legal question for the trial Judge becomes: **Is the evidence of A's past encounters with homeless men who twice assaulted and robbed her in the**

Stand Your Ground—
TO KILL, OR NOT TO KILL...

parking lot *admissible* **in her defense?** Evidence of the prior assaults, while clearly admissible to show the authenticity of A's actual, subjective, fear of an imminent assault and robbery by B, **may or may not** be admissible as to the **reasonableness** of that belief.[13]

In *People v. Goetz* (1986) 68 N.Y.2d 96, 506 N.Y.S.2d 18, 497 N.E.2d 41, the appellate Court held that the defendant should have been allowed to introduce evidence at trial of prior instances of being attacked on a subway. Defendant was charged with shooting and wounding three of four youths who had approached him on a subway and asked for $5.00. In *People v. Minifie* (1996) 13 Cal.4th 1055, 56 Cal. Rptr.2d 133, 920 P.2d 1337, defendant's conviction was reversed and remanded to the trial court for a new trial. The *Minifie* Court held that at trial a defendant in a criminal prosecution may present evidence of prior threats to the defendant by the victim's family or

---

[13] Her honest belief, however, **would** constitute "**imperfect** self-defense" so as to defend against the murder charge and have the offense reduced to Voluntary Manslaughter. In *People v. Humphrey* (1996) 13 Cal.4th 1073, 56 Cal.Rptr.2d 142, 921 P.2d 1, the Supreme Court of California held that the doctrine of imperfect self-defense applies to situations where a defendant actually believes in the need to defend against imminent death or great bodily injury, but the belief is objectively **unreasonable**. An honest albeit unreasonable belief of the need for deadly force to defend against imminent peril to life or great bodily injury negates malice aforethought, such that the offense of Murder will be reduced by the trier of fact to Voluntary Manslaughter. *People v. Blakely* (2000) 23 Cal.4th 82, 96 Cal.Rptr.2d 451, 999 P.2d 675; *People v. Rodriguez* (1997) 53 Cal.App.4th 1250, 62 Cal.Rptr.2d 345.

Scenario Four

associates, in order to show that **the defendant's fear was reasonable**. Moreover, where a victim has previously threatened a defendant, the defendant is entitled to **act more quickly and to take sterner measures** of self-defense than one who has not been threatened. *People v. Torres* (1949) 94 Cal.App.2d 146, 151, 210 P.2d 324. However, it has been held that a person cannot justify his acts on the ground of self-defense by evidence of previous incidents which were **entirely independent** of the assault with which the person is charged, involving **unrelated assailants**. *People v. Gaeta* (1960) 176 Cal.App. 830, 3 Cal.Rptr. 384; *People v. Montgomery* (1911) 15 Cal.App. 315, 114 P.2d 155.

Sticks and clubs are within the class of weapons which may be considered deadly weapons. *Allen v. United States* (Ark. 1895) 157 U.S. 675, 15 S.Ct. 720, 39 L.Ed. 854. Had A used *non*-deadly force against B (such as pepper spray with the transitory effect of temporary blindness and extreme discomfort), a jury might be more inclined to be liberal in its determination that a reasonable person might have shared A's belief in imminent harm. However, in a homicide case, such latitude, from a practical standpoint, seems less likely. Also, of course, there is the related question of whether A's use of **deadly force** was reasonably necessary to repel the attack. In a prosecution for assault with a deadly weapon, danger of a lesser degree than great bodily injury will not justify the use of deadly force to repel the attack.

Stand Your Ground —
TO KILL, OR NOT TO KILL...

People v. Lopez (1948) 32 Cal.2d 673, 197 P.2d 757.

B was in fact unarmed and there is nothing to indicate that A mistakenly perceived B to be armed with any weapon. Nevertheless, deadly force may be utilized even where the attacker is **unarmed**, if such deadly force is reasonably necessary to repel the attack due to a **gross disparity in size** [*Willingham v. State* (1955) 262 Ala. 550, 80 So.2d 280; *Hinson v. State* (Miss. 1969) 218 So.2d 36], **health** [*State v. Fetzik* (RI 1990) 577 A.2d 990], **multiple assailants** [*Allen v. United States* (1895) 15 U.S. 675, 15 S.Ct. 720, 39 L.Ed. 854; *State v. Pearson* (1975) 288 N.C. 34, 215 S.E.2d 598], **fighting experience or the violent nature of an attack** [*Hinson v. State, supra*]. The size and strength of the assailant, as well as his reputation for violence, are facts upon which the party assailed may judge his or her danger. *Cooper v. State* (Ohio 1930) 170 N.E. 355, 121 Ohio St. 562. If a person's physical disadvantage to the assailant effectively precludes an effective weaponless resistance, that person may utilize a weapon to resist a public whipping. *State v. Bartlet* (Mo. 1902) 71 S.W. 148, 170 Mo. 658.

To avoid being beaten up, it was lawful for a person to arm himself with a **pump handle** or similar weapon in order to gain an advantage over the deceased. *State v. Goodwin* (Mo. 1917) 195 S.W. 725, 271 Mo. 73. In *State v. Bowling* (Tenn. 1880) 3 Tenn. Cas. 110, 3 Shan. 110, the defendant was being held by the hair with his head forced down by a man of

Scenario Four

unusual strength and ferocity. The man was beating defendant with his fist unmercifully when defendant shot him. It was held by the Tennessee Supreme Court that defendant's claim of self-defense was a complete defense to the charge. Similarly, in *Morrison v. State* (Tenn. 1963) 371 S.W.2d 441, 212 Tenn. 633, the Court held that deadly force was justified in self-defense where the victim, a man intoxicated and of great strength, with a reputation for being rough and a fighter, broke into the dwelling house of defendant who was a much smaller, weaker and older man. Where there exists a **large disparity of physical size or power,** death or great bodily injury may be inflicted by an aggressor's hands or feet. Accordingly, the right to use deadly force may apply as against an unarmed but physically imposing aggressor. *Doswell v. State* (Ala. App. 1949) 42 So.2d 480, 34 Ala.App. 546.

The **more prudent approach** for A would have been for her to have been **more aware** of her surroundings and to have **verbally warned** B to stay a distance away from her **before he was so close** that her immediate and precipitous action was required. Also, A might have been able to retreat to the safety of her vehicle had she been more aware of her surroundings. Alternatively, A could have brandished the stick weapon at a distance as a further warning without actually committing an assault. Under such circumstances, had B **continued** to have moved forward aggressively, A would likely have been entitled to use deadly force, particularly considering the

Stand Your Ground —
TO KILL, OR NOT TO KILL...

difference in gender, size and strength as between A and B.

This scenario presents a **close case** that could go either way, Guilty or Not Guilty, as to perfect self-defense, depending in part upon whether the jurisdiction does or does not allow evidence of **prior independent events** on the question of the reasonableness of A's belief. Whether deadly force was reasonably necessary would likewise be a close call in a Murder or Voluntary Manslaughter prosecution in this case. A prosecutor might argue, on this point, that a **lesser** degree of force, such as striking B with the stick to his legs, might have been sufficient. However, in the real world, given the disparity in size between A and B, and the close proximity of B's associates, A's use of deadly force would likely be viewed as reasonably necessary so long as A's fear of imminent, deadly force, harm was objectively reasonable.

Finally, if this scenario took place in a State where there was a **duty to retreat** (discussed elsewhere in this book) prior to the use of self-defense, a jury might find A to have had a **completely safe retreat into her vehicle**, thus depriving her of the defense of self-defense. On this issue, however, it would appear that when discovered, the apparent threat imposed by B was **too close in physical proximity** to afford A a "completely safe" retreat into her vehicle, thus obviating the duty to retreat legal prerequisite for the use, by A, of deadly force.

Scenario Five
Mutual Combat

Facts: A, a 60 year-old man in good physical fitness for his age, with a legitimate[14] black belt in karate, is snoozing on a bench in the County park on a Saturday afternoon. An errantly thrown football lands directly next to him. B, a 20 year-old college student of similar size and stature to A, jogs over to retrieve his football and to apologize for the ball startling A. A, still rattled from the ball hitting so closely to him tosses the football into a nearby lake, telling B, "There's no football playing in the County park." A local regulation in this County park does forbid the throwing of footballs, baseballs or plastic saucers or rings inside the park. B tells A to retrieve his football from the lake, "or there's going to be trouble." A responds by advising B to screw off, then stands and tells B, "If you want to throw down, then let's go right here,

---

[14] Legitimate in the sense that he is an actual expert in self-defense for his age and physical stature, as opposed to having received a black belt from a karate "mill" where the training is substandard and the operative factor is money-for-belt.

Stand Your Ground—
TO KILL, OR NOT TO KILL...

right now." B then lunges at A, attempting to kick him, but A blocks the kick and knocks B down. B jumps up and punches A in the nose, breaking it. Police arrive and break up the fight. County Sheriff's officers arrest A and B, who are each later charged with battery and disorderly conduct. Both A and B sue each other civilly for damages resulting from their respective injuries.

Analysis: Although B acted in clear and indisputable violation of the County regulation forbidding the throwing of footballs in the park, an analysis of the **legislative history** of this regulation would reveal that it was intended to protect visitors from harm caused by thrown footballs, baseballs or plastic saucers and rings, and from being trampled by the people who are attempting to catch such objects. There is no indication that the Ordinance was intended to protect against **fights** resulting from erratically thrown objects. Moreover, there would certainly be no provision for a ***private citizen* enforcing** the regulation by discarding a thrown football into a nearby lake, for example.

In this case, A is not justified in taking the law into his own hands and his actions of tossing the football into the lake provoke B's conditional threat that if A refuses to retrieve the football, there's going to be trouble. An assault in a **civil** sense is either an attempted battery or a **threatened unlawful imminent**

Scenario Five

battery with a present ability to make good on the threat. Thus, in a **civil law** context, since B does not have the right to demand that A wade into the lake and retrieve the football, his conditional threat, coupled with his proximity to A and B's ability to immediately assault A, constitutes a civil assault. A civil assault could give rise to "general" monetary damages of pain and suffering arising from the threat, "special" damages for out-of-pocket losses such as medical costs or lost earnings, and punitive monetary damages (to set an example and deter future similar conduct) because assault is by definition an "intentional tort."

A **escalates** the verbal argument by telling B to screw off, or other words to that effect. Still, no physical contact has occurred to this point and neither party has actually attempted to batter the other. Thus, to this point there is neither a battery, nor, **in a** *criminal* **law sense**, an assault (an attempted battery). **Then, the corner is turned.** When A in effect invites B to engage in **mutually** consented to combat ("If you want to throw down, then let's go right here, right now."), and B responds by lunging at A, the two persons have engaged in **unlawful mutual combat**. In legal effect, there has been an "agreement" between the two of them to engage in unlawful combat.

The general rule is that anyone engaging in mutually consented to combat has **waived the right to claim self-defense**. In *People v. Ross* (2007) 155 Cal.App.4th 1033, 1046, 1056, 66 Cal.Rptr. 438, a

Stand Your Ground —
TO KILL, OR NOT TO KILL...

California Court of Appeal considered a scenario wherein a defendant who punched an assailant after being slapped in the face was convicted of aggravated assault and battery. The Court ruled that the trial Court committed prejudicial error by improperly suggesting in a jury instruction that the doctrine of mutual combat might apply to **any and every** exchange of blows, thus preventing a defendant from asserting a right to self-defense. In so ruling, the Court explained that "mutual combat" means,

> "...fighting by mutual intention or consent, as most clearly reflected in an express or implied agreement to fight. The agreement need not have all the characteristics of a legally binding contract; indeed, it necessarily lacks at least one such characteristic: a lawful object. But there must be evidence from which the jury could reasonably find that both combatants actually consented or intended to fight before the claimed occasion for self-defense arose."

In a Tennessee case, the facts were somewhere between mutual combat and the defendant being the initial aggressor. There, a defendant traveled to the victim's home, argued with the victim and refused to leave and invited the victim to get his gun. When the victim walked back toward defendant with a gun, defendant shot and killed the victim. Under these circumstances, the Court in *Gann v. State* (Tenn. 1964) 383 S.W.2d 32, 214 Tenn. 711 held that a claim of self-

Scenario Five

defense was not available to the defendant.

Where parties engage in a "mutual combat," each party is **civilly responsible for the injuries caused by that party against the other** during the incident. Moreover, the fact that each party **consensually engaged** in the fight is considered to not be a defense to a civil action for damages filed by the other party. *Clondict v. Hewitt* (Wyo. 1962) 369 P.2d 278. Where plaintiff and defendant (antagonistic concerning a recent lawsuit) called each other vile names, defendant told plaintiff to get down off his horse (literally) and that defendant would give him what he needed. When an ensuing fight broke out, defendant bit off a knuckle and broke bones of one of plaintiff's fingers. The Court in *Milan v. Milan* (Wash. 1907) 90 P. 595, 46 Wash. 468 held that defendant was legally responsible for the injuries sustained by plaintiff in the mutually consented to fight.

In the instant Scenario, there is ample evidence to the effect that the fight was not simply a spontaneous exchange of blows, but was preceded by A's explicit invitation to B to engage in a fight and B's tacit acceptance of that offer by lunging at A. The "mutual combat" fight was on.

A California criminal prosecution jury instruction pertaining to the legal effect of mutual combat on the right of self-defense reads as follows:

"The right of self-defense is only available to a person who engages in mutual combat:

Stand Your Ground—
TO KILL, OR NOT TO KILL...

(1) If he has done all the following: A. He has actually tried, in good faith, to refuse to continue fighting; B. He has by words or conduct caused his opponent to be aware, as a reasonable person, that he wants to stop fighting; C. He has caused by words or conduct his opponent to be aware, as a reasonable person, that he has stopped fighting; and D. He has given his opponent the opportunity to stop fighting. After he has done these four things, he has the right to self-defense if his opponent continues to fight. (2) If the other party to the mutual combat responds in a sudden and deadly counterassault, that is, force that is excessive under the circumstance, the party victimized by the sudden excessive force need not attempt to withdraw and may use reasonably necessary force in self-defense." CALJIC 5.56 Self-Defense—Participants in Mutual Combat.

In the present case, there was no communication of any election to stop fighting between A and B. Also, there was no sudden and deadly counterassault by either A or B. Thus, both A and B would be **deprived** of any right to claim self-defense in justification for the battery on the other. Accordingly, in this Scenario both A and B would be found guilty of criminal assault and battery charges, as well as Disturbing the Peace, and the defense of self-defense would **not** be available to

Scenario Five

either of the men. In the competing civil actions, A would be civilly liable for all of the injuries sustained by B and B would be civilly liable for all of the injuries sustained by A. The football was retrieved and seized by the County Sheriff's officers and placed into public service at the next Sheriff's Officers Benevolent Association picnic.

Stand Your Ground—
TO KILL, OR NOT TO KILL...

Scenario Six
Imminent Harm
Defense of Others

Facts: A, a healthy man in his 40s, skilled in martial arts, is parking his vehicle in a crowded parking lot. He sees an open spot and begins to pull in when another vehicle, driven by B, also attempts to pull into the same spot from his left side. Each car is blocking the other from entering the parking spot. B, an elderly and frail man in his late-70s, steps out of his vehicle from the driver's door. From inside A's vehicle, A yells at B, "If you weren't such an old man, I'd bust you in the mouth." B immediately reaches into his vehicle, extracts a large hunting knife from the console and starts walking around his vehicle toward A's vehicle, stating, "That was a big mistake you young son-of-a-gun!" A's car stalls and won't restart and his driver's window is down. A steps out of the vehicle, parries the knife away from A, and punches B viciously in the stomach at which time the knife falls to the ground. A 40 year-old Filipino woman passerby, C, sees this unfold from behind B but did not see the

Scenario Six

knife. C only sees B being hit in the stomach. As she approaches, C views the knife on the ground, but does not know its origin. With B still on the ground, C picks up the knife. C is an expert in knife fighting. Holding the knife in a threatening manner but **not moving in or otherwise attempting *to cut*** A, C orders A, "Down on the ground or I'll cut you ear to ear!" A complies. Police arrive and arrest B and C for assault with a deadly weapon and A for Battery.

Analysis: A threat conditioned upon an immutable circumstance that does not actually exist cannot create a reasonable fear of imminent harm. In this case, when A yells to B that A would hit him in the mouth if B "weren't such an old man," the threat is conditioned upon B not being an old man. But B's age cannot and will not reverse, so A's verbal threat of harm cannot be considered to create a threat of "imminent" harm.

In California, in order for a homicide to be "justifiable," and therefore, lawful, the defendant must have acted "when there is reasonable ground to apprehend a design to commit a felony or to do some great bodily injury, and **imminent** danger of such design being accomplished..." (bold added for emphasis) California Penal Code Section 197(3). According to *People v. Gonzales* (1917) 33 Cal. App.340, 342, 164 P. 1131, prior threats, when not coupled with a hostile act or apparent design to carry

Stand Your Ground —
TO KILL, OR NOT TO KILL...

them into present effect, are not sufficient to constitute a reasonable fear of imminent danger. Moreover, as held in *People v. Trevino* (1988) 200 Cal.App.3d 874, 879, 246 Cal.Rptr. 357, although a defendant's anger or other emotions cannot be said to **preclude** the defense, emotions other than fear of bodily harm or the commission of a felony cannot be considered a **causal factor** in a decision to use deadly force. For example, knowledge of the fact that the wife of defendant had cheated on him in an illicit act with another did not justify defendant's killing of his wife. *People v. Vincent* (Ill. 1946) 68 N.E.2d 275, 394 Ill. 165.

Thus, in this Scenario, A's "threat" that if B were not an old man, A would "bust" him in the mouth (i.e., a threat with no apparent intent to harm B), cannot justify B in pulling a knife from his vehicle and approaching A in a menacing manner. Even B's emotional response to the insult does not add to the circumstances in support of B seeking to defend himself. A prosecution of B for assault with a deadly weapon, or of brandishing a deadly weapon, for that matter, would be successful and could not be averted by B's claim of self-defense.

Here, A's car stalled and would not restart and the window was down. B's conduct, particularly when accompanied by his verbal threat of, "That was a big mistake you young son-of-a-gun!," would likely cause a reasonable person to have an actual fear of imminent harm from B's intended use of deadly force (the knife). Because of the close proximity and immediacy of B's

Scenario Six

attack, A would have been **unable to retreat**, even if there were a duty to retreat in this jurisdiction prior to the exercise of self-defense. Thus, any prosecution of A for punching B viciously in the stomach would fail since this act is undoubtedly in self-defense, is not the result of mutual conduct, and appears to have been reasonably necessary.

When C comes onto the scene, she has no knowledge of the events prior to viewing A hit B (an older man) violently in the stomach. However, as seen above, a person is entitled to rely upon the events as he, and a reasonable person in his position, sees them. The **defense of others** is not limited to **actual** facts but to facts as the defendant, and a reasonable person in defendant's position, **perceives** them to be. C does not know where the knife came from but has viewed A punch B in the stomach. In the heat of the moment, she picks up the knife in order to protect B from further harm. Importantly, C merely holds the knife in a threatening manner and does not actually use the knife for any overt physical attack against A. C orders A, "Down on the ground or I'll cut you ear-to-ear!" A complies and does not attempt to flee or attack C.[15]

---

[15] An interesting legal enigma would have occurred had A **responded** to C's threatened deadly force by directing **deadly force against** C. In this situation of lawful self-defense versus lawful defense of others, both A and C would be acting with lawful justification and neither A nor C would be responsible for any injuries to the other. Fortunately, this unusual situation did not occur.

Stand Your Ground —
TO KILL, OR NOT TO KILL...

C's **defense** to a charge of assault with a deadly weapon is **two-fold**: (1) C made no effort to actually physically inflict harm against A with the knife, and since assault **in a criminal law sense** is an **attempted battery**, there can be no conviction here for assault with a deadly weapon[16]; and (2) as a good Samaritan, viewing the situation reasonably from the information available to her, C would argue that she was entitled to use force, or the threat of force, to defend B, as a **"defense of others."**

California Penal Code Section 693 provides:

"Resistance sufficient to prevent the offense may be made by the party about to be injured: (1) To prevent an offense against his person, or his family, or some member thereof. (2) To prevent an illegal attempt by force to take or injure property in his lawful possession."

California Penal Code Section 694 provides,

"Any other person, in aid or defense of the person about to be injured, may make resistance sufficient to prevent the offense."

---

[16] Also, the mere display of a knife to deter an onrushing attacker was not deemed deadly force in *Douglas v. United States* (DC 2004) 859 A.2d 641. The District Court in *Stewart v. State* (Fla. Dist. Ct. App. 2d Dist. 1996) 672 So.2d 865 held that the mere display of a gun without more does not constitute "deadly force" for purposes of determining whether the display of the gun is justified.

Scenario Six

In *People v. Kirk* (App. Dept. Superior Court 1986) 192 Cal.App.3d Supp. 15, 238 Cal.Rptr. 42, the Court was faced with an appeal by the defendant who had been convicted of drawing a gun in a threatening manner. The trial court had refused to give a requested instruction to the jury regarding the defense of others, although there was prima facie evidence of the reasonableness of defendant's belief that he was saving a rape victim at the time that he brandished his gun. The Court in *Kirk* **reversed**, ruling that the defendant was entitled to a jury instruction on the defense of others.

In the present Scenario, C would be entitled to claim that her brandishing of the knife was justified based upon the defense of defense of others, in order to protect B from further harm. This claim of defense would likely be successful. The fact that C did not take the time to determine the origin of the knife or whether B was in fact the aggressor would not likely control the jury's determination of whether a reasonable person in C's position would have feared for B's safety from unlawful attack. Also, as noted above, in the heat of the moment, in the face of imminent danger, a person will not be expected to perfectly gauge or nicely calculate the degree of force necessary to repel an attack, and the force used in response will not be considered unlawful unless **clearly excessive**. Here, C's brandishing of the knife and her verbal threats to compel A to stop his attack on B would most likely be deemed justified by the defense of others.

Stand Your Ground—
TO KILL, OR NOT TO KILL...

Scenario Seven
Reasonable Force
Withdrawal from the Fight

Facts: A, a healthy Asian woman in her 30s, has been training in karate and Muay Thai for three years, although she has never fought in a full-contact match. In her purse, she habitually carries a kubeton (a weapon typically composed of a rigid aluminum dowel, ½ inch in diameter and 6 inches in length) hooked to her key chain. While power-walking on a Sunday morning around 9:00 a.m. in a crowded park, she is intersected by two males, B and C, 20s, who commence flirting with her, talking to her about how sexy she is and telling her that they want to have sex with her. She firmly tells them to leave her alone and calls 9-1-1 to ask for police assistance. A extracts her kubeton from her purse as she walks. The two men, matching her pace, persist in their flirtatious and even off-color comments. Without warning, B grabs her arm roughly and she back-knuckles the man across the face. Both men then attack her as a crowd gathers

Scenario Seven

to watch. A strikes B in the mouth with her kubeton, breaking most of his front teeth. A then breaks two ribs of C with the kubeton as he charges. With the crowd cheering her on, both men back up and B exclaims, "Okay, okay, we don't want none a this, lady. Back off, we're done. It's over." B turns and walks away through the crowd. As C turns away from A to pull a knife from his pants pocket, he chimes in, "We're done lady". Not yet seeing the knife held by C, A attacks C, raking the kubeton across his face and kneeing C in the stomach, doubling him over. A then pursues B into the crowd, catching up with him and striking him with a blow to the head with the end of the kubeton which extends from her grasp. B suffers brain damage from the blow and falls unconscious. As she continues to strike the unconscious B with her fists and kicks, C runs up from behind and cuts A on her neck with the knife blade. The crowd swarms C and police arrive. A is arrested and charged with assault with a deadly weapon on B. B is transported to the hospital but is later arrested and charged with battery on A. C is arrested and charged with assault with a deadly weapon, assault with intent to kill, attempted murder and simple battery on A. B sues A in a civil lawsuit for personal injuries suffered in the attack of A by B with the kubeton.

Stand Your Ground —
TO KILL, OR NOT TO KILL...

Analysis: In this scenario, A is an experienced martial artist female who possesses a weapon in her purse known as a kubeton. Although small, if used to its potential a kubeton can easily inflict great bodily injury and lethal force. Unlike pepper spray, the effects of which are transitory, the harm inflicted by a kubeton in skilled hands can be **horrendous, lasting and deadly**. Like a sap or a baton, a kubeton is undeniably a deadly weapon.

A is confronted by two men who walk along side her and make unwanted flirtatious remarks, which were understandably unsettling to A. However, in a crowded area, the flirtatious and even off-color remarks from the two men, as a matter of law, are not such that a reasonable person in A's position would believe that physical harm was imminent. Nor do they rise to the level of even a simple battery such as in the case, for example, of the finger poking in the movie theater scenario referred to above. Words or gestures, as we have seen, however abusive or insulting, if not otherwise constituting a threat of imminent harm, will **not** justify as self-defense the use of force against the verbally abusive person. Moreover, as held in *People v. Valencia* (2008) 74 Cal. Rptr.3d 605, 180 P.3d 351, mere sexual overtures will not in themselves support a murder defendant's perfect or imperfect self-defense claim.

At a critical point in the walk, one of the two men, C, grabs one of A's arms roughly. This is clearly a battery, since it constitutes a harmful or offensive touching,

Scenario Seven

and this battery justifies A in defending herself with force reasonably necessary to repel the battery. In this case, there are two men and one of her, but it is in a crowded park during the day and all of these factors would come into play in determining the **level of force** which would be considered reasonable in response to the unwanted grab of A's arm. Were it at night in an isolated corner of a parking garage, a **heightened level of risk** would give rise to a heightened level of force which could reasonably be used in response. However, where a defendant is assaulted by multiple rioters, the defendant may **act more quickly and with greater forcible means** to protect himself and family than had he been assaulted by a single assailant. *Higgins v. Minaghar* (Wis. 1891) 47 N.W. 941, 78 Wis. 602.

When A back-knuckles B to B's face, this use of force should be deemed entirely reasonable under the circumstances. However, then the two men up the stakes and both attack her. A is out-weighed and out-manned. Faced with an actual assault by two grown men and despite the fact that other people are around, A does not know whether anyone will come to her aid and in fact, no one does come to her aid. Based upon the legal authority discussed above, and in view of the disparity in size and number of assailants, A would be justified in using a much higher level of force in response to the two-man attack in process. Moreover, A doesn't have a mere **fear** of an imminent attack, an imminent attack by the two men is **actually underway**.

Stand Your Ground —
TO KILL, OR NOT TO KILL...

As the United States Supreme Court stated in *Brown v. United States* (1921) 256 U.S. 335, 41 S.Ct. 501, 65 L.Ed. 961,

> "Detached reflection cannot be demanded in the presence of an uplifted knife."

When A breaks most of B's teeth with the kubeton and breaks C's ribs with a kubeton strike, she has arguably used force likely to cause great bodily injury. These strikes, however, were measured strikes and not to vital areas. Most likely, under the circumstances, these early kubeton strikes would be viewed as constituting reasonable levels of force to repel the attack.

After the initial blows by A are struck, both men back up and B tells A that they don't want to fight, "… Back off, we're done. It's over." After communicating this termination of the affray, B turns and walks away through the crowd. C also tells A that they are finished, but C does **not** walk away, and instead turns to pull a knife from his pocket.

A defendant who initiates a wrongful attack and then has a need to use force to defend himself or others as a result of the conflict, cannot claim self-defense (or the defense of others) as a defense to a battery or homicide prosecution. *Felker v. State* (1891) 54 Ark. 489, 16 S.W. 663; *Hulse v. Tollman* (1893) 49 Ill. App. 490; *People v. Miller* (1882) 49 Mich. 23, 12 N.W. 895; *State v. Porter* (1953) 238

Scenario Seven

N.C. 735, 78 S.E.2d 910. However, where a danger has **passed** because the attacker has **withdrawn** and has **communicated** this withdrawal to the victim, the general rule is that there is no justification for the use of further or additional force against the initial attacker. *People v. Parrish* (1985) 170 Cal.App.3d 336, 217 Cal.Rptr. 700; *People v. Smith* (1981) 122 Cal.App.3d 581, 176 Cal.Rptr. 73; *People v. Evans* (1969) 2 Cal.App.3d 877, 82 Cal.Rptr. 877. A person who approached the decedent's gin in order to burn it, but fled upon being discovered, did not lose his right to exercise self-defense, including the use of deadly force as reasonably necessary, since he had abandoned his intent to destroy property. *Felker v. State* (Ark. 1891) 16 S.W. 663, 54 Ark. 489. Thus, when an aggressor withdraws in good faith from the conflict and communicates in some manner this withdrawal to his opponent, but the opponent continues the physical altercation, the initial aggressor may then lawfully defend himself under the claim of self-defense. *Rowe v. United States* (1896) 164 U.S. 546, 41 L.Ed. 547, 17 S.Ct. 172; *State v. Kennedy* (1915) 169 N.C. 326, 85 S.E. 42; *Banks v. State* (1971) 51 Wis.2d 145, 186 N.W.2d 250.

In the present case, it would appear that B genuinely (i.e., in "good faith") intended to withdraw from the conflict. B communicated this benign intent to A, turned and walked away in the crowd. C, on the other hand, did not move away and it is not clear whether his purported communication ("We're done

Stand Your Ground—
TO KILL, OR NOT TO KILL...

lady.") of an intent to withdraw was in good faith. In fact, C did **not** withdraw but instead surreptitiously pulled a knife. Although it would be a factor for consideration that A did not actually *see* C pull the knife, the fact that C was a **recent aggressor** and was **not moving away from A** would strongly support A's belief that C still constituted an imminent threat of deadly force. Under the circumstances, and in the heat of the moment, it is likely that A was justified in continuing her attack on C. A reasonable person in A's position would not be required to **wait to be stabbed** or further accosted by her attacker before taking further steps in self-defense.

Within the concept of self-defense is a defender's prerogative known as a **right of attack**. Where the accused has a reasonable belief that the deceased intends to kill him or cause him great bodily harm and that that intention will be accomplished, the accused **need not wait** until the deceased gets an advantage over him. In such circumstances the accused **may preemptively attack**, and kill, the aggressor if necessary to avoid the danger. *State v. Matthews* (Mo. 1899) 49 S.W. 1085, 148 Mo. 185. Accord, *State v. McGee* (Mo. 1950) 234 S.W.2d 587, 361 Mo. 309 (right of attack requires necessity, real or apparent, and an imminent danger or the reasonable appearance of danger). When defendant is aware, for example, that an armed man is seeking to shoot him, defendant may act immediately in self-defense, without waiting for the assailant to draw his weapon, aim and pull the trigger.

Scenario Seven

This is the rule so long as the danger is imminent and there is neither a safe retreat nor some other reasonable manner in which to avoid the danger. *State v. Connally* (Or.Cir. 1869) 3 Or. 69.

Thus, after B departs the scene, and before C attempts to use the knife against A, A need not wait to defend herself. When A rakes the kubeton across C's face and knocks the air out of him with a knee to the stomach, this force against C would likely be deemed legally justified in self-defense.

Unfortunately for A and for B, A does not stop there. It is true that a person who is attacked may pursue his attacker until he is safe from danger, but this is only true if that course is reasonably necessary as it would appear to a reasonable person in those circumstances. *People v. Hughes* (1951) 107 Cal. App.2d 487, 237 P.2d 64; *People v. McDonnel* (1949) 94 Cal.App.2d 885, 211 P.2d 910; *People v. Moody* (1943) 62 Cal.App.2d 18, 143 P.2d 978.

B has in good faith communicated an actual intent to withdraw from the conflict, and he attempted to leave the scene. While A may have been entitled to make a **citizen's arrest** on B, this is **not** what she attempted to do. When A caught up to B, the force applied against B was anything but reasonable.

When A strikes B to the head with her kubeton, B falls unconscious, having suffered serious brain injury. Without a doubt, this kubeton hit constitutes the use

Stand Your Ground —
TO KILL, OR NOT TO KILL...

of deadly force since it is likely to cause great bodily injury (in this case, lasting brain damage) or death. With the crowd cheering her on, A **continues to strike the unconscious B** with punches and kicks.

The defense of self-defense is not available where, although a defendant may have been in reasonable fear of harm when he first beat the victim, the victim was unconscious as the defendant continued the attack. *People v. Shade* (1986) 185 Cal.App.3d 711, 716, 717, 230 Cal.Rptr. 70. In *People v. Barber* (N.Y.A.D. 4 Dept. 2000) 703 N.Y.S.2d 328, 269 A.D.2d 758, the aggressor victim was lying face down with gunshot wounds to his leg and chest and posed no continuing threat of imminent harm to the defendant. When defendant nevertheless shot him at close range to the back of his head, the Court ruled that no instruction on self-defense was required to be given to the jury. On the other hand, in *Huber v. United States* (9th Cir. 1919) 259 F. 766, 170 C.C.A. 566, 4 Alaska Fed. 763, the Court commented that defendant had been wrong in tossing the deceased's blankets out of defendant's cabin and ordering him to get out. However, where defendant was thereafter attacked, shoved into his own bunk and choked by the decedent to the edge of defendant being "all in," defendant was legally justified in using reasonably necessary force, including killing the decedent, to protect himself from death or great bodily injury.

A's merciless attack on the withdrawing B was at

Scenario Seven

its outset the unjustified use of force since B no longer represented an imminent threat of harm to A. B was withdrawing, not attacking, and B had communicated this intention to A. As set forth in *Rowe v. United States*, cited above, B had withdrawn from the fray and was departing through the crowd when hit in the head with the kubeton strike by A. When B is unconscious, of course, he cannot be said to represent any threat whatsoever to A, and each of the subsequent strikes to B constitutes the application of unlawful force by A. Had B regained consciousness, B would have had the right to defend himself with deadly force against A's attack.

At this time and under these circumstances, C arrives at the scene and cuts A's neck to attempt to stop her from continuing to unlawfully assault B. Where a person without a right of self-defense is confronted by **an escalation of the violence** through *"a sudden and deadly force"* (italics added for emphasis), he is then entitled to defend himself against that application of deadly force. *People v. Heckler* (1895) 109 Cal. 451, 42 P. 307. C's use of deadly force against A to defend B would arguably constitute reasonable force in defense of others against A's **unlawful** application of deadly force against B. C's cutting A with the knife would likely result in a Not Guilty verdict for C in view of the defense of necessity known as the defense of others.

A was arrested for assault with a deadly weapon on B and aggravated battery with great bodily injury to B.

Stand Your Ground —
TO KILL, OR NOT TO KILL...

Under the facts of this Scenario, once A continued her attack on B after he had withdrawn from the fray, the defense of self-defense would no longer have been available to A and she would be unable to claim self-defense for her deadly force attack against B.

B's civil lawsuit against A for injuries suffered by B after B had withdrawn would be successful, and costly to A. B would be entitled to recover damages for pain and suffering, "special damages" for present and future medical expense and for present and future loss of earnings, and punitive damages for malice. Since the attack was willful, any civil damages would not be dischargeable in bankruptcy. [Title 11, United States Code, Section 523(a)(6) (intentional tort)]. Finally, B and C would both be found guilty on criminal charges for their initial acts in attacking A prior to B's withdrawal from the conflict.

Scenario Eight
Battered Person Syndrome
Imminent Harm

Facts: A, a 35 year-old woman, is married in a common law marriage to B, a man in his 50s. A has been repeatedly battered by B, with resulting chronic serious bodily injury to A, over the past 15 years of their relationship. After each battery, B pleads for forgiveness and apologizes profusely, and A eventually forgives B, and reconciles with him. Then the cycle repeats, again and again. One Sunday dinner, A burns a pot roast and B beats her severely. Hours later, B goes to sleep. A siphons gasoline from their car parked in the garage, douses the bedroom with the gasoline and sets the house on fire, killing B in the process. A is arrested for and charged with premeditated First Degree Murder. In an interrogation, A admits to police that while B was sleeping, B was no **immediate** threat to A, but through the tears, A manages to state,

> "You don't know what it was like. He beat me severely, over and

Stand Your Ground —
TO KILL, OR NOT TO KILL...

over, year after year. It was only a matter of time."

When then asked by police, "**What** was only a matter of time?", she responds, "Before he killed me."

Analysis: It is axiomatic that, and as set forth above, a claim of self-defense **must** be based upon the element of an **actual** and **objectively reasonable** fear of *imminent* harm, real or apparent. For example, a paramour may, if reasonably necessary, kill his lover's husband in lawful self-defense if he has a reasonable belief that the husband is about to kill him or cause him great bodily injury. *Woodson v. State* (Ariz. 1926) 247 P. 1103, 30 Ariz. 448.

However, a threat of force to occur in **the distant future** (e.g., even several hours later) will generally not constitute an **imminent** threat of force since the person threatened presumably has the time and ability to seek protection from law enforcement officials in the interim period of time. In *United States v. Bello* (1st Cir. 1999) 194 F.3d 18, the federal Court of Appeals held that no self-defense instruction was required to be given to the jury where the defendant prisoner committed an assault in a prison recreational area **18 hours after** receiving a threat from the victim. The Court reasoned that in the interim period, defendant, "could have reported the incident to the guards and requested the protection they were required to

Scenario Eight

provide..." Similarly, in *United States v. Haynes* (7th Cir. 1998) 143 F.3d 1089, a federal Court of Appeals held that no right of self-defense existed where the threat of force by another inmate was "of action later that afternoon" and where defendant was not faced with an imminent use of force.

However, as pointed out by legal scholars, the issue should not be,

> "...the immediacy of the threatened harm, but the **immediacy of the response necessary in defense**. If a threatened harm is such that it cannot be avoided if the intended victim waits until the last moment, the principle of self-defense must permit him to act earlier – as early as is required to defend himself effectively." 2 P Robinson, Criminal Law Defenses, Sect. 131(c)(1) (1984).

These circumstances most commonly arise in the context of a battered spouse or a chronically abused child. In a so-called **"battered person syndrome,"** a wife (although it could also be a husband, child or other dominated and chronically abused person) has been subjected to a cycle wherein the spouse repeatedly batters her, inflicting serious bodily and psychological injury. Then, the aggressor spouse begs for forgiveness and seeks love and comfort, whereupon the battered spouse reconciles, and the cycle repeats itself over and over. The battered spouse

Stand Your Ground —
TO KILL, OR NOT TO KILL...

is relegated to a position of helplessness, with no relief in sight. In the battered person syndrome, the wife may realize that her husband will eventually kill her and it's only a question of when that killing will occur.

In most jurisdictions today, expert testimony is permitted to prove up the circumstances of battered person syndrome as a justification for a **seeming modification** to the requirement of imminent harm. *See*, for further discussion, Dressler, *Battered Women and Sleeping Abusers: Some Reflections*. 3 Ohio St. J. Crim. L. 457 (2006).

Although not a defense in itself *per se*, the battered person syndrome is relevant to the defense of self-defense. *People v. Hartman* (N.Y.A.D. 3 Dept. 2009) 883 N.Y.Supp.2d 361, 64 A.D.3d 1002. The California Supreme Court, in *People v. Humphrey* (1996) 13 Cal.4th 1073, 56 Cal.Rptr.2d 142, 921 P.2d 1 held that a defendant's personal situation and knowledge are relevant in determining both the defendant's subjective honesty **and the objective reasonableness** of her actions. Citing California Evidence Code Section 1107 (adopted in 1991), allowing expert witness opinion testimony about battered spouse syndrome in criminal trials, the Court held that, in the face of all of the evidence, **including** the expert witness testimony,

"The jury must consider defendant's situation and knowledge, which makes the evidence relevant, but the ultimate question is

Scenario Eight

whether a reasonable person, not a reasonable battered woman, would believe in the need to kill to prevent imminent harm. Moreover, it is the **jury**, not the expert, that [sic: which] determines whether defendant's belief and ultimately, her actions, were objectively reasonable." (13 Cal.4th at 1087)

However, in Ohio, the rule is different. There, the test pertains to the **mind of the accused**, such that the issue becomes whether the **accused's** state of mind is on reasonable grounds, not whether a hypothetical "reasonable person" would have had such a belief. *State v. Reid* (3rd Dist. Allen County 1965) 210 N.E.2d 142, 3 Ohio.App.2d 215. Accordingly, an obsequious, nervous or easily intimidated person would not be measured by the same standard by which a tougher, more experienced or braver person might be judged. *Nelson v. State* (4th Dist. Athens County 1932) 181 N.E. 448, 42 Ohio App. 252.

In the present Scenario, A would be entitled to introduce expert testimony in support of her own testimony about the repeated and unrelenting abuse she suffered at the hands of B, and in support of the reasonableness of her subjective belief that if she did not do something to kill her husband, it was only a matter of time before he killed her. Her statements to police under interrogation would be consistent with this defense and admissible as prior consistent statements of the accused. Similar statements by A,

Stand Your Ground —
TO KILL, OR NOT TO KILL...

also admissible in evidence, would presumably be made by A later to **mental health experts** in the case. Under the stipulated facts of this Scenario, it is likely that A's claim of self-defense would be successful and that A would be acquitted of the crime of Murder.

Scenario Nine
Actual Harm Versus Perceived Harm
Defense of Others

Facts: A pulls into a parking lot when he notices an argument in progress in which B is demanding money from C. A observes B striking C in the face and knocking C to the ground. B picks up two one-hundred dollar bills from the ground. C starts to get up but B kicks him. A walks up behind B and, with an inward handsword to the neck, knocks B unconscious. C runs off but A remains at the scene of the crime and calls 9-1-1. Police arrive and interview B. Police discover that B had just been robbed by C when B defended himself against C, attempting to both stop the robbery and get his money back. B further explains that at that moment, B was struck from behind by an unknown person. A admits to police that he was the person who struck B from behind, but claims it was in justifiable defense of B's attack on C. A is arrested for and charged with battery and robbery.

Stand Your Ground —
TO KILL, OR NOT TO KILL...

Analysis: Aiding and abetting is accomplished if someone does something to knowingly and affirmatively aid, encourage or facilitate the commission of a crime. *See, e.g.*, California Penal Code Section 31. Here, there is no evidence beyond mere (false) speculation that A knew that a robbery was in progress. After striking B, A remained at the scene and called 9-1-1 for police to come to the scene. This behavior is not reasonably consistent with being a participant in C's robbery of B. Accordingly, any prosecution of A for robbery would fail.

Also, as discussed above, a claim of self-defense is not limited to those situations in which an **actual** threat of harm exists. In a **majority** of jurisdictions, a person may in good faith properly defend himself with reasonable force (even if their perception of the events is mistaken) **when a reasonable person in the same or similar circumstances would also have believed that actions in self-defense were necessary to avert imminent harm**.[17] The rule is the same, of course, for the defense of others. *State v. Menila* (1916) 177 Iowa 283, 158 N.W. 645 (defendant killed her husband in the reasonable **but mistaken** belief that the husband

---

[17] In a minority of jurisdictions, the defender is put in the shoes of the person being defended. This so-called **"alter ego" rule** allows a defense of others defense only if the person defended would have been entitled to assert self-defense. *People v. Young* (1962) 11 N.Y.2d 274, 229 N.Y.S.2d 1, 183 N.E.2d 319 (defendant guilty of battery for using non-deadly force against a plain clothes police officer effecting a lawful arrest); *Batson v. State* (1997) 113 Nev. 669, 941 P.2d 478

Scenario Nine

was about to kill their son).

However, some American statutes still purport to limit the use of force in defense of others to the defense of persons with **some designated relationship** with the defender. In *Haines v. State* (Okla. Crim. App. 1954) 275 P.2d 347, 1954 Ok. C.R. 85, a statute permitted the use of reasonable force in defense of a husband, wife, parent, child, master, mistress or servant. The defendant killed an assailant of defendant's extra-marital lover and sought to assert the defense of defense of others. *Haines* held that the statutory defense (21 O.S. 1951 Sect. 733) of defense of others did not justify deadly force in defense of an **unlawful relationship amounting to that of a paramour and concubine**.

California Civil Code Section 50 ostensibly limits that necessary force may be used to defend the person or property of, "...oneself, or of a wife, husband, child, parent, or other relative, or member of one's family, or of a ward, servant, master, or guest." However, at least in a criminal law context, other California statutes allow for the exercise of defense of others **without regard to any relationship** (e.g., Penal Code Sections 692 through 694).

("one who would come to the defense of others must stand in the shoes of the person being defended"); *Leeper v. State* (Wyo. 1979) 589 P.2d 379 (defendant in the shoes of her husband who had no right of self-defense because he engaged in mutual combat with the victim). The **gross shortcomings of the alter ego rule** are cogently described in *State v. Fair* (1965) 45 N.J. 77, 211 A.2d 359, 369.

Stand Your Ground —
TO KILL, OR NOT TO KILL...

These broader statutes are consistent with the better rule that no particular relationship with a person about to be attacked is required in order for a defender to be entitled to the "defense of others" legal defense. *Williams v. State* (1943) 70 Ga.App. 10, 27 S.E.2d 109 (stranger); *State v. Totman* (1899) 80 Mo.App. 125 (bystander); *State v. Fair* (1965) 45 N.J. 77, 211 A.2d 359 (despite restrictive statute requiring special relationship, self-defense allowed where defending a friend). In *Fair*, the court wrote that not only, as a matter of justice, would one,

> "...not be convicted of a crime if he selflessly attempts to protect the victim of an apparently unjustified assault, but **how else can we encourage bystanders to go to the aid of another who is being subject to assault**." (bold added for emphasis)

Accord, *Fersner v. United States* (1984 DC App) 482 A.2d 387. In *State v. Beeley* (RI 1995) 653 A.2d 722, defendant assaulted a naked man in the apartment of defendant's friend when he found that man fighting with a friend. The Court held that defendant was entitled to a jury instruction which exonerated him if the jury found that he reasonably believed, under the circumstances as appeared to him, that his friend was entitled to self-defense, even if, in fact, the friend was not the victim but rather was the aggressor regarding a man sleeping with his wife.

In the present Scenario, A is presented with a

Scenario Nine

situation which is, from all reasonable appearances, a robbery in progress. A sees B striking C and then picking up two one hundred dollar bills. C starts to get off the ground and B kicks him. Although many people would not get involved in this sort of a situation, as a Good Samaritan A takes it upon himself to step in to protect C from further harm and in doing so, knocks B unconscious with a chop to the neck (a very effective strike). This is not deadly force since there is no lasting injury and the strike is generally not likely to cause great bodily injury or death. C runs off. A has no particular relationship with C and the question arises **whether A may lawfully "defend" C in any event since there is no prior relationship between A and C**. In those minority of jurisdictions requiring a relationship such as a family relationship or co-habitation, A's conduct will not be justified as defense of others. But the better and majority rule is that no such relationship is required for a defense of others claim.

However, there is still the matter of C having been the initial aggressor in this scenario and so the next issue becomes **whether A could lawfully intervene on the reasonable, but mistaken, honest belief that B was the aggressor and not C**. In the minority of jurisdictions which require a defender to "step in the shoes" of the person defended, A would be in trouble and would not be entitled to an acquittal based upon a defense of others defense. (One would hope that the prosecutor, in his prosecutorial discretion, would elect

Stand Your Ground—
TO KILL, OR NOT TO KILL...

not to prosecute such a violation.) However, again, the better and majority rule is that A should be entitled to act in honest belief upon reasonable appearances. In such case, any prosecution of A for battery on B would likely fail since A has a complete defense of others claim of defense, despite the fact that C was the actual aggressor against B.

Scenario Ten
Defense of Property
Deadly Force

Facts: A, 20s, a physically fit male, trained in mixed martial arts, is a guest of X at X's home. When X leaves to purchase some beer and pizza for an upcoming, televised MMA event, B, an intruder, male, 30s, physically fit, enters a partially enclosed front porch of X's residence. B expects to enter the residence with the intent to commit theft inside the residence (a felony known as "Burglary"). Before B can make it inside the residence, however, A exits the house and confronts B on the porch. B has no burglary tools in his possession, but spontaneously exclaims to A, "I thought everyone was gone, man. Hey, I was just gonna rob the place, it's all cool." A immediately attacks B, taking him onto the floor, crushing his windpipe, dislocating his shoulder, breaking his left arm at the elbow and thumb-gouging one of his eyes to the point where it would cause permanent blurring and the disfigurement of a "lazy" eye. When X arrives home and discovers B injured on the porch, he calls the police and

Stand Your Ground —
TO KILL, OR NOT TO KILL...

requests that paramedics be dispatched. X later confirms to the police that he does not know B and had never given B permission to enter his front porch or home. A explains to the police the facts of what transpired when B entered the porch, and states that he feared that B would attack him in order to safely flee the scene. The police arrest B for trespass and paramedics transport him to a hospital. A is arrested for and later charged with assault with force likely to cause great bodily injury and for battery on B. B sues A in a civil suit for excessive force and A responds by filing for Chapter 7 bankruptcy protection.

Analysis: B's expressed intent was to enter X's home and burglarize[18] it. In response, it is absolutely clear that A used "deadly" force against B. Recall that force need not cause death in order to constitute deadly force. Deadly force is force likely to cause death **or great bodily injury**. Great bodily injury is defined in California, for example, as "a significant or substantial physical injury." California Penal Code

---

[18] Robbery is theft from a person by force or threat of force. Burglary is entry into a structure, or into a locked vehicle, with the intent to commit theft or any felony inside. Although B copped to intending to "rob the place," it's clear that what he **meant** was that since he thought everyone had left the premises, he was going to burglarize the structure by entering it with the intent of committing theft therein.

Scenario Ten

Section 198.5. Great bodily injury has been defined elsewhere as injury of,

> "...the type of force that creates a high probability of death, results in serious disfigurement, results in loss of any member or organ of the body or results in permanent prolonged impairment of the use of any member or organ of the body." *State v. Lucero* (2010) 147 N.M. 747, 228 P.3d 1167.

In the present case, A used his mixed martial arts training to accomplish **devastating** injury to B, insofar as he took him down to the floor, crushed his windpipe, dislocated his shoulder, broke his left arm at the elbow and gouged his eye. Moreover, the injury to the eye turns out to be **permanent disfigurement and blurring of vision**. These injuries, amount to an *overwhelming case* of the use of deadly force.

In general, the **common law** rule is that deadly force cannot be used solely for the protection of property. *People v. Ceballos* (1974) 12 Cal.3d 470, 116 Cal.Rptr. 233, 526 P.2d 241. A mere trespass on open land, even with prior warning, does not justify the use of deadly force. Where defendant lay in wait and shot and killed the victim who was 30 feet away quietly passing through the premises of another, along a trail, the killing was neither justified as defense of property nor as self-defense. *State v. Schieler* (Idaho 1894) 37 P. 272, 4 Idaho 120. In *Carpenter v. State* (Ark. 1896) 36 S.W. 900, 62 Ark. 286, the Court held that a defendant

Stand Your Ground —
TO KILL, OR NOT TO KILL...

may not lawfully defend against a mere trespass by killing the trespasser to protect an agricultural crop. In *State v. Trent* (Or. 1927) 259 P. 893, 122 Or. 444, a man lawfully driving along a public highway stopped and entered defendant's melon patch. Believing that the man intended to steal melons from the melon patch, defendant killed him. *Trent* held that the killing was not in justifiable defense of property. A defendant/landlord was not entitled to claim self-defense or defense of property where the defendant attempted to evict a tenant by "smoking" them out of the premises. In *Gedye v. People* (Ill. 1897) 48 N.E. 987, 170 Ill. 284, the Court held that where defendant had obstructed the chimney thereby forcing smoke throughout the house and defendant was thereupon met by resistance of the tenant and tenant's son, defendant was not justified in responding to such resistance by killing the son who had attacked defendant. In *People v. Capello* (Ill. 1918), 118 N.E. 927, 282 Ill. 542, a policeman hopped onto a wagon to inspect a case of beer being transported from a railway station in an "anti saloon" territory. The driver/defendant responded with lethal force. In *Capello*, the Court held that the driver had no defense of property right to kill the officer to prevent a trespass. Indeed at least in some jurisdictions, **no force at all** can be used to protect against simple interference with property unless a request is made that the person desist. *State v. Cessna* (1915) 170 Iowa 726, 153 N.W. 194.

Following the common law, in California, an owner

Scenario Ten

of property may exercise reasonable force to protect against the **immediate** danger of it being taken, destroyed or substantially harmed by another who has no lawful claim of immediate possession. *People v. Flanagan* (1881) 60 Cal. 2; *see also, Goshen v. People* (1896) 22 Colo. 270, 44 P. 503. However, an owner of personal property may not, on claim of defense of property, take it from the peaceful albeit wrongful possession of another by the use of force. *Barnes v. Martin* (1862) 15 Wis. 240. In *Singleton v. Townsend* (La.App.4 Cir. 1976) 339 So.2d 543, defendant shopkeeper was informed that $4 worth of gasoline had not been paid for. In an ensuing high speed car chase, defendant fired five shots at plaintiff's automobile. The *Singleton* Court held that defendant's conduct constituted **excessive force** and was not justifiable as a defense of property. In *Kinder v. Commonwealth* (Ky. 1936) 92 S.W.2d 8, 263 Ky. 145, the Court held that the killing of a person in order to prevent a simple theft cannot be justified as defense of property. *Kinder* reasoned that in order for a killing to be justified, the offense sought to be prevented must threaten the security of a person or home or contain an element of force or violence.

In *Crouch v. Ringer* (Wash. 1920) 188 P. 782, 110 Wash. 612, a customer had returned fish which she believed and claimed were bad. She was given a full refund by the shop owner. Subsequently, the customer ignored the shop owner's explicit instruction to leave the shop and instead, followed him around,

Stand Your Ground —
TO KILL, OR NOT TO KILL...

talking excitedly. *Crouch* held that the under the circumstances, the shop owner/defendant could use any reasonably necessary force to eject the customer/plaintiff from the premises after she received the refund.

However, at common law when a perpetrator entered or sought to destroy **a man's home**, it was considered an assault **against the man himself**. Accordingly, an owner or resident of the home **could** defend against such an intrusion with whatever force as was reasonably necessary to repel the attack. *Hall v. State* (Ark. 1914) 168 S.W. 1122, 113 Ark. 454. When the property which an owner seeks to protect is **inside a home**, a greater degree of force may be permissible in the defense of property. *Wilson v. State* (1892) 30 Fla. 234, 11 So. 556; *State v. Perkins* (1914) 88 Conn. 360, 91 A. 265. Under the so-called "Make My Day Law," defendant could use deadly force against an intruder who broke into a home in which defendant was an invited visitor. *State v. Anderson* (Okla. Crim. App. 1998) 972 P.2d 32, 1998 Ok.C.R. 67.

If the home is entered, or attempted to be entered, under circumstances as to create a reasonable belief that the owner's life is in jeopardy or that the intruder intends to commit a felony, such owner may use deadly force, if reasonably necessary, to prevent or terminate such entry. *Hickey v. United States* (9th Cir. 1909) 168 F. 536; *People v. Dann* (1884) 53 Mich. 490, 19 N.W. 159; *Morgan v. Durfee* (1879) 69 Mo. 469.

Scenario Ten

In *Beard v. United States* (1895) 158 U.S. 550, 15 S.Ct. 962, 39 L.Ed. 1086, a defendant, on his own premises, killed his assailant who had threatened to assault him. The United States Supreme Court, in *Beard*, stated,

> "[T]he question for the jury was whether, without fleeing from his adversary, he had, at the moment he struck the deceased, reasonable grounds to believe, and in good faith believed, that he could not save his life or protect himself from great bodily harm except by doing what he did."

In modern jurisprudence, in a majority of jurisdictions, if an intruder enters someone's home, **it is presumed** that the use of deadly force in stopping that intrusion constitutes the exercise of reasonable force. For example, California Penal Code Section 198.5 creates a presumption that a person who used deadly force within his residence reasonably feared imminent danger of death or great bodily injury to himself, his family or a household member.

Actual entry by the assailant into the home **is required**, however, before the presumption applies. *People v. Brown* (1992) 6 Cal.App.4th 1489, 1495, 8 Cal.Rptr.2d 513 (entry by the victim onto an **unenclosed front porch** does not constitute entry into the residence); *People v. Curtis* (1994) 30 Cal.App.4th 1337, 1362, 37 Cal.Rptr.2d 304 (the presumption of the reasonableness of the use of deadly force does

Stand Your Ground —
TO KILL, OR NOT TO KILL...

not arise unless there is actual entry). The right to defend one's castle with reasonable force including, as reasonably necessary, **deadly** force does not extend, however, to the **center of the street in front** of the "castle." *State v. Boyd* (S.C. 1923) 119 S.E. 839, 126 S.C. 300. The Castle Doctrine exemption from the duty to retreat, and the associated presumption of the reasonableness of the use of deadly force does not apply to a fatal confrontation occurring in defendant's **driveway**, instead of in his home itself. *Connecticut v. Carlino* (Mass. 1999) 710 N.E.2d 967, 429 Mass. 692.

Similarly, in the New York case of *People v. Bennett* (N.Y.A.D. 4 Dept. 1995) 623 N.Y.S.2d 59, 212 A.D.2d 1028, the Court held that an **open porch** was not part of defendant's "dwelling," for purposes of determining whether defendant had a duty to retreat rather than use deadly physical force. However, in Washington, a person outside his own dwelling house has no duty to retreat from an attack by a person with a deadly weapon and may defend himself using reasonably necessary force. *State v. Cushing* (Wash. 1896) 45 P. 145, 14 Wash. 527.

In the California statutory scheme, a presumption of the reasonableness of the use of deadly force is applicable only to a **resident** of the home. A guest, even if allowed to occasionally stay overnight, is not entitled to the presumption. *People v. Silvey* (1997) 58 Cal.App.4th 1320, 1326, 68 Cal.Rptr.2d 681.

Scenario Ten

In a "duty to retreat" State, A may also have to overcome the requirement that before exerting deadly force upon another, he retreats if a completely safe retreat is reasonably available to him. In this case, A could have stepped back through the back door to retreat (*see, People v. Aiken* (N.Y. 2005) 828 N.E.2d 74, 795 N.Y.Supp.2d 158, 4 N.Y.3d 324, *infra*), and thus A may, in certain jurisdictions, be unable to claim defense of property or self-defense in any event.

Florida also has a form of the so-called **"Castle Doctrine."** This doctrine in Florida is **so comprehensive and detailed** it is worth quoting the underlying statute in full. Florida Statutes Section 776.013 reads:

> "(1) A person is presumed to have held a reasonable fear of imminent peril of death or great bodily harm to himself or herself or another when using defensive force that is intended or likely to cause death or great bodily harm to another if: (a) The person against whom the defensive force was used was in the process of unlawfully and forcefully entering, or had unlawfully and forcibly entered, a dwelling, residence, or occupied vehicle, or if that person had removed or was attempting to remove another against that person's will from the dwelling, residence, or occupied vehicle; and (b) The person who uses defensive force knew or had reason to

Stand Your Ground—
TO KILL, OR NOT TO KILL...

believe that an unlawful and forcible entry or unlawful and forcible act was occurring or had occurred.

(2) The presumption set forth in subsection (1) does not apply if: (a) The person against whom the defensive force is used has the right to be in or is a lawful resident of the dwelling, residence, or vehicle, such as an owner, lessee, or titleholder, and there is not an injunction for protection from domestic violence or a written pretrial supervision order of no contact against that person; or (b) The person or persons sought to be removed is a child or grandchild, or is in the lawful custody or under the lawful guardianship of, the person against whom the defensive force is used; or (c) The person who uses defensive force is engaged in an unlawful activity or is using the dwelling, residence, or occupied vehicle to further an unlawful activity; or (d) The person against whom the defensive force is used is a law enforcement officer...who enters or attempts to enter a dwelling, residence, or vehicle in the performance of his or her official duties and the officer identified himself or herself in accordance with applicable law or the person using force knew or reasonably should have known that the person entering or attempting to enter was a law enforcement officer.

Scenario Ten

(3) A person who is not engaged in an unlawful activity and who is attacked in any other place where he or she has a right to be[19] has no duty to retreat and has the right to stand his or her ground and meet force with force, including deadly force if he or she reasonably believes it is necessary to do so to prevent death or great bodily harm to himself or herself or another or to prevent the commission of a forcible felony.

(4) A person who unlawfully and by force enters or attempts to enter a person's dwelling, residence, or occupied vehicle is presumed to be doing so with the intent to commit an unlawful act involving force or violence.

---

[19] The Castle Doctrine in Florida has been extended by judicial interpretation to protect persons in their **place of employment** while lawfully engaged in such employment, so long as the assailant is not their co-worker. *Frazier v. State* (Fla. Dist. Ct. App. 2d Dist. 1996) 681 So.2d 824. It also applies to a person's **place of business**. *State v. Bobbitt* (Fla. 1982) 415 So.2d 724. The language of subsection (3) of "…and who is attacked in any other place where he or she has a right to be" could be construed to apply to a park, a sidewalk, an amusement park, or a beach, for example, but most likely would not include the **presumption** that deadly force was in play but instead would be limited to the "no duty to retreat and has the right to stand his or her ground" provision. Deadly force could still be used "if he or she reasonably believes it is necessary to do so to prevent death or great bodily harm to himself or herself or another or to prevent the commission of a forcible felony." This would be true at common law and the **added** aspect is that there is no duty to retreat in Florida and a person may under such circumstances stand his ground and meet force with like force. In this regard, Florida law is virtually identical to the law of a majority of States in the United States, including, notably, California.

Stand Your Ground —
TO KILL, OR NOT TO KILL...

(5) As used in this section, the term: (a) 'Dwelling' means a building or conveyance of any kind, including any attached porch, whether the building or conveyance is temporary or permanent, mobile or immobile, which has a roof over it, including a tent, and is designed to be occupied by people lodging therein at night. (b) 'Residence' means a dwelling in which a person resides either temporarily or permanently or is visiting as an invited guest. (c) 'Vehicle' means a conveyance of any kind, whether or not motorized, which is designed to transport people or property."

Thus, in Florida, the Courts have uniformly held that where a person, who is not the aggressor, is violently attacked in his home, the person so attacked need not retreat and may use such force as reasonably appears to be necessary to protect himself. *Falco v. State* (Fla. 1981) 407 So.2d 203; *Unis v. State* (Fla. Dist. Ct. App. 4th Dist. 1998) 717 So.2d 581. Even a hotel room, rented by the defendant for the night, qualified in Florida as a dwelling for purposes of the Castle Doctrine governing the justifiable use of force. *Stieb v. State* (Fla. Dist. Ct. App. 2d Dist. 2011) 67 So.3d 275.

In the present case, A does not live in the home and accordingly, in some jurisdictions the presumption of reasonableness of the use of deadly force would not arise. In Florida, however, the presumption of reasonableness of the use of deadly force may arise

Scenario Ten

since A was an invited guest in the residence. Also, in some jurisdictions, B would not be considered to have actually entered the home at the time of being attacked by A. He had entered the partially enclosed patio. There is no indication that B had to break into the patio and a reasonable inference is that the patio does not have an exterior door with a lock (since it is "partially enclosed"). Accordingly, in some jurisdictions, including California, such a patio would not be considered to be **inside** the home for purposes of application of the presumption. In Florida, however, an attached porch with a roof over it **is** within the statutory definition of a Dwelling, but it must be unlawfully and forcibly entered in order for the deadly force presumption to arise. Here, the attached porch was not entered by force; B simply walked onto it without use of force.

Even if a presumption arises that deadly force is reasonably necessary in responding to an intruder unlawfully entering a residence, this presumption **can be overcome by countervailing evidence**. It is a mere presumption, not a **conclusive** presumption. For example, in the instant Scenario, B was unarmed and, once confronted by A, B made no overt effort to enter the dwelling itself nor to attack A. Also, A was a skilled martial artist and once the physical confrontation commenced, it would have been obvious to A that he could overwhelm and control B quickly and probably without the use of deadly force. Thus, in the instant Scenario, even if the presumption arose,

Stand Your Ground—
TO KILL, OR NOT TO KILL...

it could arguably have been overcome at trial by the prosecution.

Without a presumption, however, **proof** of the reasonableness of the use of deadly force against the intruder **becomes even more difficult**. The issue is whether the facts and circumstances, as known to A, (and not aided by any legal presumption) would have been sufficient such that a reasonable person would believe that deadly force was reasonably necessary to repel an imminent attack.

Here, although B intended to enter the residence, he had no burglary tools that might be used as a weapon. B said or did nothing to indicate that he was a highly trained empty-hands fighter or that he had any insidious design against A. To the contrary, B stated, upon seeing A emerge from the residence, that "...it's all cool." Finally, B was given neither a warning nor an opportunity to leave the partially enclosed porch. Even if you assume moreover, for purposes of argument, that A was reasonable in his apprehension that B was on the verge of assaulting A, that would still not justify the use of deadly force to subdue B. In order for self-defense, or even the defense of property, to be legally justified, it must be *a reasonably necessary level of force*. In the present case, the force itself was **grossly excessive** and the defense of self-defense, or the defense of property, would not be available to A. A's defense to the criminal charges would almost certainly be **unsuccessful**.

Scenario Ten

Moreover, when B sued A in **civil** court, the indisputable fact that the level of force was excessive would prevent A from defending the lawsuit on the basis of self-defense or defense of property. Accordingly, a substantial monetary judgment would be likely in B's favor and against A to compensate B for general damages of pain and suffering, special damages of medical bills and future medical expense and of loss of earnings and earning capacity, and punitive damages for the intentional tort of assault with force likely to cause great bodily injury, among other torts. A bankruptcy filing would not help A, since as noted previously, Judgments based upon intentional torts are not dischargeable in bankruptcy.

Stand Your Ground—
TO KILL, OR NOT TO KILL...

Scenario Eleven
No Duty to Retreat

Facts: A, an 18 year old male Honors student in high school, Brown Belt in Karate and track letterman sprinter of slight build is warned by B, an All-League but somewhat lumbering high school defensive lineman, not to walk past B's parent's home again. A had broken up with B's sister, Y, a week before and Y ran away for two nights in despair before returning home. B cautions A that if A walks past B's house, B intends to "take care of you for good. **You'll never walk again.**" Previously, B had been suspended from school for beating up another student, X, two years younger and fifty pounds lighter than himself, over a dispute concerning where each of the two boys wanted to hang out on campus during lunch time. A was aware of this incident, since X was a friend of A's younger sister, Z. The route past B's home is the most direct way for A to return home from school. The very next day, A **ignores** B's warning and walks by B's parents' home. Seeing A walk by, B steps

Scenario Eleven

outside of the house **carrying a tire iron**, and advances **menacingly** toward A. B yells out to A, "You asked for this! Now you're **really** gonna get it!" In actual fear for his life, A pulls a concealed gun from his book bag and shoots B in the chest one time, killing him instantly. At the time of the shooting, B was only ten feet away from A and was closing the distance rapidly. When police arrive, A is arrested for and later charged with the murder of B. A is also expelled from his high school and sued by B's parents for wrongful death.

Analysis: Despite the fact that A is a Brown Belt in karate, the legal question is **not** whether *alternative* means of defending oneself would have been reasonably available. A defendant may use **whatever** force is reasonably necessary to repel an unlawful attack. *Acers v. United States* (1896) 164 U.S. 388, 41 L.E. 481, 17 S.Ct. 91; *Spencer v. State* (1887) 77 Ga. 155, 3 S.E. 661; *Miers v. State* (1895) 34 Tex.Crim. 161, 29 S.W. 1074. In the instant case, since A was **actually** in fear for his life, the legal issue is whether the **use of a gun** constituted reasonable force in repelling the attack. Asked another way: would a reasonable person in the position and circumstances of A have believed that his or her life was in imminent danger when B, an All-League tackle in high school who had previously warned A to stay clear of B's house or he'll "never walk again," advanced menacingly toward and within 10 feet of A with a tire iron in his hands.

Stand Your Ground—
TO KILL, OR NOT TO KILL...

The general rule is that a person may not use a dangerous weapon in self-defense if the assailant is not armed. *Davis v. State* (1898) 152 Ind. 34, 51 N.E. 928; *Shields v. State* (1925) 187 Wis. 448, 204 N.W. 486. Prior experiences of assaults or threats are admissible to show the reasonableness of one's belief in the need to use deadly force to repel an attack. Where evidence exists showing that the defendant was afraid of the victim, testimony regarding the victim's character and reputation for violence is admissible and relevant to show **the objective reasonableness** of defendant's fear. *E.B. v. State* (Fla. Dist. Ct. App. 3d Dist. 1988) 531 So. 2d 1053; *Burk v. State* (Fla. Dist. Ct. App. 2d Dist. 1986) 497 So.2d 731. In this case, the evidence of B's prior, similar, assault on X would typically be admissible in A's favor on the issue of the fact and reasonableness of A's belief in an imminent threat of deadly force from B.

A could arguably have avoided the confrontation altogether by choosing a different route home, or by walking with friends, or by calling the police, or by informing school authorities. However, a person has no duty to **curtail his activities** to avoid an encounter with someone who has threatened to attack. As held by the California Supreme Court in *People v. Gonzales* (1887) 71 Cal. 569, 12 P. 783:

> "For one may know that if he travels along a certain highway he will be attacked by another with a deadly weapon, and be compelled in self-defense to kill his assailant,

Scenario Eleven

and yet he has the right to travel that highway, and is not compelled to turn out of his way to avoid the expected unlawful attack." (71 Cal. at 578)

In the present case, B was armed and physically capable of carrying out the attack, with a clear motive for and a previously expressed purpose of harming A. He was closing the distance in a menacing manner towards A. B had a reputation of violent behavior against younger, smaller students. Under these circumstances, **any reasonable person in A's same or similar circumstances would clearly be in fear for his life or of great bodily injury.** Thus, **unless A was under a legal obligation at any time to** *retreat*, he was legally justified in extracting his concealed firearm (carrying a concealed weapon without an applicable concealed weapon permit would be a separate crime) and shooting to kill.[20] A may have reasoned with B prior to or during the attack or even run away.

---

[20] Experts agree that shooting to wound or "wing" someone is virtually always ill-advised. Attempting to shoot a moving target in an arm or leg is highly difficult under the intense pressure of the moment, and even if successful, may not accomplish the goal of stopping the attack. Law enforcement and military are trained to shoot two shots to the body core followed by one shot to the head when firing upon an armed and dangerous person. The exception would be if the perpetrator was wearing body armor, in which case law enforcement would shoot lower and to the head.

Stand Your Ground—
TO KILL, OR NOT TO KILL...

Many conceivable scenarios may have avoided the attack. **But was A *legally responsible* to retreat?**

In English "common law," a person generally had a duty to retreat if reasonably safe prior to the exercise of self-defense. A fascinating **historical view** of the development of the common law as to self-defense is chronicled in *Sydnor v. State* (2001) 776 A.2d 669, 365 Md. 205, and quoted in pertinent part within the APPENDIX to this book.

In modern times in the United States, the **majority** of States have case law and statutes supplanting common law and establishing that a person ***need not retreat*** but may instead ***stand his ground*** and use whatever force is reasonably necessary to defend himself. *See, e.g., Beard v. United States* (1895) 158 U.S. 550, 39 L.Ed. 1086, 15 S.Ct. 962; *Rowe v. United States* (1896) 164 U.S. 546, 41 L.Ed. 547, 17 S.Ct. 172; *Miller v. State* (Wis. 1909) 119 N.W. 850, 139 Wis. 57. In *State v. Gardner* (1905) 104 N.W. 971, 96 Minn. 318, the Court commented on the antiquated origins of the duty to retreat laws,

> "The doctrine of 'retreat to the wall' had origins **before the general introduction of guns**...[I]t would be rank folly to...require [retreat] when experienced men, armed with repeating rifles, face each other in an open space, removed from shelter, with an intent to kill. Self-defense has not, by statute nor [sic: or] by judicial opinion, been distorted, by

The Legal Limits of Safety

Scenario Eleven

an unreasonable requirement of the duty to retreat, into self-destruction." (104 N.W. at 975)

Under what is known in Tennessee as the "True Man Doctrine," a person is under no obligation to retreat from a place where he has a lawful right to be and he may defend himself from threatened attack despite the fact that he could safely retreat. *State v. Renner* (Tenn. 1995) 912 S.W.2d 701. This was the result of a 1989 Legislative prerogative in Tennessee to move away from the common law duty to retreat rules. The *Renner* Court cautioned however that,

> "...[A]s in all cases of self-defense, the force used must be reasonable, considering all of the circumstances. Moreover, the 'true man' rule implies no license for the initiation of a confrontation or an unreasonable escalation of a confrontation in progress." (912 S.W.2d at 704)

See also, Boykin v. People (Colo. 1896) 45 P. 419, 22 Colo. 496 (tendency of modern cases is to greatly modify the common law rule re: "retreat to the wall" concept); *People v. Toler* (Colo. 2000) 9 P.3d 341 (true man doctrine still available to a **trespasser** who does **not** have a right to be where he is at when he has a need to defend himself from unlawful imminent force).

When defendant is completely without fault,

Stand Your Ground —
TO KILL, OR NOT TO KILL...

defendant need not retreat but may stand his ground and repel the attack by force, including deadly force, if necessary. *Foote v. Com.* (Va. App. 1990) 396 S.E.2d 851, 11 Va.App. 61. *See also*, to this effect, *People v. Smith* (Ill. 1949) 88 N.E.2d 834, 404 Ill. 350 and *Wade v. State* (Miss.App. 1998) 724 So.2d 1007 (defendant may stand his ground if in a place where he has a right to be and is not the aggressor).

In Florida, there is never a duty to retreat before using **non-deadly** force. *Keith v. State* (Fla. Dist. Ct. App. 1993) 614 So.2d 560. However, EFFECTIVE October 1, 2005, Florida statutory law established that **wherever a person has a right to be** he may stand his ground and use **deadly force**. Currently, Florida statutory law provides that a person **has no duty to retreat and may meet force with force**, **including deadly force**, if he reasonably believes it to be necessary to prevent death or serious bodily injury to him or to another, or to prevent the commission of a forcible felony. Fla. Stat. Sect. 776.013(3).

In Oklahoma, before using deadly force to repel an attack of deadly force, the defendant **must take reasonable steps to avoid the danger**. However, he **is not obligated** *to retreat* to avoid the danger, so long as he is in a place wherein he has a lawful right to be and has done no wrongful act to bring the assault upon him. *Turner v. State* (Okla. Crim.App. 1910) 111 P. 988, 4 Okla. Crim. 164. There is no duty to retreat when a person is assaulted in a place where he has a lawful

The Legal Limits of Safety

Scenario Eleven

right to be. *State v. Jordan* (Wash.App.Div. 1 2010) 241 P.3d 464, 466, 158 Wash.App. 297.

In California, a person who is attacked may stand his ground and defend himself, if necessary, even by the use and application of deadly force. *People v. Newcomer* (1897) 118 Cal. 264, 273, 50 P. 405; *People v. Maughs* (1906) 149 Cal. 253, 260, 86 P. 187; *People v. Dawson* (1948) 88 Cal.App.2d 85, 198 P.2d 338. In *Dawson*, the Court of Appeal wrote:

> "Where an attack is sudden and the danger imminent, one may increase his danger by retreat. In such case he may stand his ground and slay his attacker, **even though it be proved that he might have more easily gained safety by flight**." (88 Cal.App.2d at 95; bold added for emphasis)

Similarly, in Florida, a person has no duty to retreat and may use deadly force if he reasonably believes that deadly force is necessary to prevent imminent death or great bodily harm to him or to another or to prevent the imminent commission of a specified list of forcible felonies. Fla. Stat. Sect. 776.012(1).

If there is no duty to retreat before resorting to self-defense, however, the **possibility of escape** is one **factor** in determining whether defendant's use of deadly force was reasonably justified. *State v. Brown* (La. 1982) 414 So.2d 726. However, even in a duty to retreat State, to overcome a defense of self-defense

Stand Your Ground—
TO KILL, OR NOT TO KILL...

by the user of deadly force, the prosecution must prove **beyond a reasonable doubt** not only that a retreat with complete safety was **objectively possible**, but also that defendant **subjectively was aware** of such manner and means of retreat. *People v. Soriano* (N.Y.A.D. 1 Dept. 2007) 828 N.Y.Supp.2d 369, 36 A.D.3d 527.

Even in a State where there is a general duty to retreat prior to the exercise of self-defense, if an attack is **so fierce and imminent** that the party attacked is reasonably justified in subjectively believing that he *cannot* retreat **without increasing the inherent danger** (i.e., there is no "completely safe retreat"), then he may stand his ground and use deadly force, if reasonably required to repel his assailant. *State v. Meyer* (Wash. 1917) 164 P. 926, 96 Wash. 257. Where defendant's wife advanced upon him in their home wielding a butcher's knife, defendant had no duty to retreat before using reasonable force, including deadly force, to protect himself from harm. *State v. Grantham* (S.C. 1953) 77 S.E.2d 291, 224 S.C. 41.

Accordingly, in this Scenario, A had no duty to take an alternate route home from school. A was entitled to arm himself with a weapon in order to defend against the anticipated attack. So long as A had no duty to retreat once confronted with the attack by B with the tire iron, A was entitled to use the gun to kill B. If a duty to retreat applied as the law of this jurisdiction, then a factual question for the jury in the criminal case

Scenario Eleven

would be whether a **completely safe retreat** (such as A outdistancing B by running away) would have been reasonably possible and known to plaintiff. In this case, the possibility of being hit by a thrown tire iron would probably have eliminated flight as being a completely safe retreat.

In most jurisdictions, even a civil suit by B's family against A would fail because A was within his lawful rights of self-defense and B was the attacking aggressor. The **school suspension** of A for carrying a gun from school (circumstantial evidence and A's later truthful admission upon school official inquiry) would stick. In school administrative proceedings, a suspension would not be so much an issue of self-defense than an issue of zero-tolerance of weapons at school.

Stand Your Ground—
TO KILL, OR NOT TO KILL...

Scenario Twelve
Wrongdoers

Facts: Staring down the barrel of a handgun, a Clerk at a liquor store, hands over cash from the register to a Robber in the course of a robbery. When the Robber is momentarily distracted by the movement of an overhead fan, Clerk pulls a shotgun from under the counter. Fearing imminent harm from Clerk's shotgun, and before Clerk can pull the trigger, Robber shoots Clerk in the chest, miraculously missing Clerk's vital organs but causing Clerk to discharge the shotgun off target. Robber takes the money from the register and flees the scene. Clerk survives to identify Robber as the shooter, and store videotape confirms that Robber was robbing Clerk at the time of the shooting. A familiar face in the neighborhood, Robber is soon arrested for and charged with assault with a deadly weapon, battery and robbery, but tells the police, "The man was gonna shoot me. I had to do it. I had to or I'd be dead right now." At trial, as to the first two

Scenario Twelve

charges, Robber claims his shooting of Clerk had been self-defense against Clerk's trying to shoot him with a shotgun. The trial court Judge, however, refuses to instruct the jury on the law of self-defense. Defendant is convicted of robbery, assault with a deadly weapon ("ADW") and battery. Defendant appeals his ADW and battery convictions, claiming he was deprived of due process by the trial court's refusal to allow his claim of self-defense.

Analysis: During the course of the robbery, the Clerk pulled a shotgun and was on the verge of shooting the Robber. There is little doubt that Clerk intended to use the shotgun against Robber, and that Robber was **completely reasonable** in his belief that in order to repel Clerk's imminent attack with deadly force, deadly force would have to be used in response. Robber pulled the trigger but, luckily, missed Clerk's vital organs, and Clerk testifies against him at trial on all counts. In a general sense, Robber acted in "self-defense": If Robber had not shot Clerk, then Clerk almost certainly would have shot Robber. **But did this shooting of the Clerk constitute a lawful use of force in self-defense?**

Generally, if a **victim** has a right to defend himself, a defendant has no right of self-defense against any reasonable force used by the victim in the victim's self-defense. *People v. Watie* (2002) 100 Cal.App.4th

Stand Your Ground —
TO KILL, OR NOT TO KILL...

866, 124 Cal.Rptr.2d 258. In *Watie*, defendant went to his mother's house to retrieve her belongings after she fled the home following a dispute with the victim. At the home, defendant argued with the victim through a security gate, threatened and challenged the victim to a fight and attempted to enter the house several times. Believing the victim to have a firearm, defendant fired his own gun into the home, killing the victim. The Court held that the refusal to instruct the jury on self-defense was correct. A defendant whose use of force provokes a violent response cannot claim a right of self-defense. *State v. Douglas* (Wash.App. Div. 2 2005) 116 P.3d 1012, 128 Wash.App. 555.

A California Court of Appeal held that the victim had the right to defend himself in his residence, and accordingly, defendant had no right of self-defense even if the victim possessed a weapon. In *People v. Smith* (1973) 33 Cal.App.3d 51, 108 Cal. Rptr. 698, the Court wrote,

> "One who assails another and then brings on an attack may not claim self-defense as a ground of exemption from the consequences of killing his adversary." (33 Cal.App.3d at 68)

The California Supreme Court in *People v. Bolton* (1979) 23 Cal.3d 208, 215, 152 Cal.Rptr. 141, 589 P.2d 396 considered a case where the trial court had refused to instruct the jury on the right of self-defense. The undisputed facts at trial were that the defendant had unlawfully pointed a gun at her husband. *Bolton*

Scenario Twelve

held that the trial court was correct in refusing the requested jury instruction. When her husband reached for his gun, **defendant was legally obligated to retreat**, and was not entitled to use force in self-defense.

In an early Oklahoma case, the defendant was not entitled to claim self-defense where defendant trespassed on the deceased's property. Carrying a repeating rifle, defendant approached the deceased's horse. The deceased reasonably believed that defendant intended to harm him, the deceased attempted to protect himself and the defendant shot the deceased. *Reed v. State* (Okla. Crim. App. 1909) 103 P. 1042, 2 Okla Crim. 589. Where a defendant departed a tavern, retrieved a shotgun from his car trunk, loaded it and returned to the tavern, **he became the aggressor** and lost his right to self-defense. *Sykes v. State* (Wis. 1975) 230 N.W.2d 760, 69 Wis.2d 616.

Where a defendant unlawfully ordered a Wyoming peace officer in Colorado to hold up his hands, the Court in *Pearson v. People* (Colo. 1917) 168 P. 655, 69 Colo. 76 held that the defendant could not claim self-defense as to his acts in overcoming the peace officer's resistance. In *State v. Turner* (Minn. 1973) 203 N.W.2d 539, 295 Minn. 539, a defendant and two friends aggravated motorists when they squirted the motorists with a water pistol. Defendant left the scene, armed himself and returned. One of the perturbed motorists spotted the defendant, gave chase, approached defendant's driver door, unarmed, and grabbed

Stand Your Ground —
TO KILL, OR NOT TO KILL...

defendant through the window. Defendant then fired two shots at the man, striking and killing him. *Turner* held that defendant was properly convicted and did not act in self-defense.

An interloper who, by his sexual advances with the defendant's wife, generates the conflict with the husband, is **precluded** from asserting a right of self-defense as a justification for a related homicide. *Dabney v. State* (Ala. 1897) 21 So. 211, 113 Ala. 33, 59 Am.St.Rep. 92. Similarly, where defendant provoked an encounter, arranged for the meeting and shot the decedent three times with a shotgun at point blank range while decedent sat in a vehicle, the defense of self-defense was not available. *Daniel v. Comm'r of Corrections* (Conn. App. 2000) 751 A.2d 398, 57 Conn.App. 651. In the case of *In re Christian S* (1994) 7 Cal.4th 768, 773, fn 1, 20 Cal.Rptr.2d 33, 872 P.2d 574, the Court held that where a defendant creates circumstances by which an adversary's attack or pursuit is legally justified, the defendant may not invoke the self-defense doctrine. In *State v. Lucero* (N.M. 1988) 972 P.2d 1143, 126 N.M. 552, the Court held that a defendant shooting a gun in the air was provocation such that defendant could not thereafter claim self-defense against a rival gang member in an ensuing gun battle.

However, in *State v. Bristol* (Wyo. 1938) 84 P.2d 757, 53 Wyo. 304, the Court set limits on depriving an accused a claim of self-defense. In *Bristol*, an accused

Scenario Twelve

had an altercation with the deceased, thereafter armed himself, and went to a restaurant where the deceased was sitting. When the accused stopped momentarily at the booth of the deceased, the deceased glared at him and then attacked the accused. The accused in turn killed the deceased. The Court held that the issue of self-defense turns on whether the accused's conduct at the restaurant was **reasonably calculated to provoke the deceased into attacking the accused**.

Under New York law, self-defense to a **robbery** permits a person to respond with deadly force to threatened force which is not itself deadly. *Lebron v. Mann* (2d Cir. 1994) 40 F.3d 561. It has been held that the use of deadly physical force to defend against attempted **forcible sodomy** is a ground for justification **independent** of the use of physical force to protect against harm from the imminent use of deadly force. *People v. Coleman* (N.Y.A.D. 4 Dept. 1986) 504 N.Y.S.2d 949, 122 A.D.2d 568. The Supreme Court of Washington held that a person may defend himself, his person and his property against another who commits or attempts to commit a violent felony such as murder, robbery, rape, arson or burglary since due to the atrocity of such offenses **it may be presumed** that human life is in peril. *State v. Nyland* (Wash. 1955) 287 P.2d 345, 47 Wash.2d 240.

In *Bonie v. State* (Fla. Dist. Ct. App. 1st Dist. 1999) 27 So.3d 88 the Court held that a defendant may **not** avail himself of the defense of self-defense if he is

Stand Your Ground —
TO KILL, OR NOT TO KILL...

engaged in, attempting, committing or escaping after the commission of a forcible felony. Moreover, the defense of justification by self-defense has been ruled to be inapplicable to a charge of attempted robbery. *People v. Ellison* (N.Y.A.D. 2 Dept. 1991) 573 N.Y.S.2d 202, 175 A.D.2d 846. A person who commits or attempts to commit a robbery armed with deadly force and in the course thereof kills the intended victim when such victim responds with the application of force to the robbery attempt, may not claim or otherwise assert the defense of self-defense. *United States v. Thomas* (2d Cir. 1994) 34 F.3d 44. If a trier of fact finds that the defendant was a participant in an attempted armed robbery before any gunshots were fired, it is **immaterial** whether the victim or defendant shot first. *People v. Guraj* (N.Y.Supp. 1980) 431 N.Y.S.2d 925, 105 Misc.2d 176. A defendant and his accomplices entered and attempted to rob a bank armed with guns. A cashier opened fire on robbers, and defendant, one of the robbers, shot and killed the cashier. At trial defendant claimed self-defense. The Court, in *State v. Hart* (Mo. 1922) 237 S.W. 473, held that under such circumstances, no self-defense had been shown, regardless of the fact that the cashier had shot the first shot.

In the present case, Robber was in the course of robbing the liquor store clerk when Clerk seized the opportunity to pull a shotgun to defend against the robbery. At that moment, Robber was **legally obligated to retreat** and could **not** lawfully use **any** force, much

Scenario Twelve

less deadly force, to defend himself against being shot by Clerk. When Robber instead shoots Clerk under these circumstances, Robber's use of deadly force was not a lawful exercise of self-defense, and was not legally justified. Robber's conviction of battery and assault with a deadly weapon would be affirmed on appeal (the robbery charge was not appealed).

Stand Your Ground —
TO KILL, OR NOT TO KILL...

Scenario Thirteen
Mutual Combat
Escalation of Force

Facts: A and B, two middle-aged men, are working out in the weight lifting area of a sports club. An argument erupts over the use of a machine used for squats and within moments, the verbal sparring escalates into a full-blown fist fight. Independent witnesses later inform police that immediately prior to the blows being thrown, A stated to B, "Bring it on!" to which B replied to A, "I'm right there." After both A and B throw punches and take some hits, B trips and falls to the ground, whereupon A suddenly grabs a nearby chrome-plated 7-pound dumbbell and lunges at B, attempting to hit him in the head with it. B reflexively snatches up a nearby steel vertical row handle and forcefully strikes A in the temple with it, killing him instantly. Videotape of the incident confirms the sequence of events. B is arrested by police for Voluntary Manslaughter. At trial, B attempts to claim a

Scenario Thirteen

right of self-defense but the trial court Judge **refuses** to instruct the jury on self-defense, and instead gives a "mutual combat" instruction. B is convicted of Voluntary Manslaughter and simple battery.

Analysis: At the outset of the fight between A and B, this scenario depicts a Mutual Combat situation, since A has invited B to fight and B has, literally, accepted the invitation. In such a fight, neither A nor B would **ordinarily** have a right to claim self-defense and each would be both criminally and civilly responsible for the injuries of the other. However, as previously described above, where a person without a right of self-defense is confronted with **an escalation of the violence** through "a sudden and deadly force," he is then entitled to defend himself against that application of deadly force.

In *People v. Heckler* (1895) 109 Cal. 451, 42 P. 307, the California Supreme Court held that where an original aggressor had not undertaken a deadly attack but rather only a simple assault or trespass, the victim has no right to use deadly or other excessive force in response. Consequently, if the victim uses deadly or other excessive force, the initial aggressor may lawfully defend himself. The Court wrote,

> "For, as his acts did not justify upon the part of the other the use of deadly means for their prevention, his killing by the other would be criminal, and one may always defend

Stand Your Ground—
TO KILL, OR NOT TO KILL...

himself against a criminal attempt to take his life."

The Court continued, holding that despite having been the initial aggressor,

> "If, however, the counter assault be so sudden and perilous that no opportunity be given to decline or to make known to his adversary his willingness to decline the strife, if he cannot retreat with safety, then as the greater wrong of the deadly assault is upon his opponent, he would be justified in slaying, forthwith, in self-defense." (109 Cal. at 464)

In *Rhoden v. Booth* (Tex.Civ.App.—Dallas 1961) 344 S.W.2d 481 the Court held that a speed wrench is not **necessarily** a deadly weapon. However, in *Hagopian v. Fuchs* (N.J.Super.A.D. 1961) 169 A.2d 172, 66 N.J.Super. 374, the Court held that a steel wedge of approximately four pounds in weight, propelled towards a person's head constitutes a "deadly weapon." In the present case, in the manner in which the dumbbell was utilized by A, it would likely be found to have been a deadly weapon under the circumstances.

In Florida, the defense of self-defense, or defense of others, is ordinarily **unavailable** to a person who initially provokes the use of force by an assailant against himself. The exceptions would be if the person withdraws from the affray and communicates to the

Scenario Thirteen

assailant his intent to terminate the use of force but the assailant nevertheless continues or resumes the use of force, **or if deadly force is applied against him by the assailant and he has exhausted every reasonable means to escape such danger other than by his own use of deadly force**. Fla. Stat. Sect. 776.041(2)(b). Where the nature of an attack is **an ordinary fist fight**, the Washington Supreme Court in *State v. Walker* (Wash. 1998) 966 P.2d 883, 136 Wash.2d 767 held that **the use of a *knife*** to fatally stab the assailant was ***not* the application of reasonable force** and a claim of self-defense could not prevail. Despite the fact that defendant was smaller in stature and had a preexisting back injury, **defendant suffered no injury** during the fist fight and no evidence existed to prove that the victim intended anything more than a common battery.

In the present scenario, A unlawfully escalated the fight from a commonplace **fist-fight** to the use of **deadly force** when he lunged at B, attempting to hit him in the head with the 7-pound dumbbell. This improvised weapon could certainly have caused death or great bodily injury if forcefully applied against B's head. This escalation of violence, moreover, was sudden, with **no reasonable opportunity for B to extricate himself** from the deadly predicament except by defending himself through the use of countervailing deadly force. Consequently, when B grabs an available weapon—a steel vertical row handle—B has a **legal right to use deadly force against A in self-defense.**

Stand Your Ground—
TO KILL, OR NOT TO KILL...

A reasonable person in B's position would likely believe that **deadly force was needed** to defend himself against A's use of deadly force.

Accordingly, at trial B was entitled **to present evidence** concerning these events giving rise to his self-defense claim. B should have been entitled to a jury instruction by the trial court concerning a right of self-defense by a mutual combatant when faced with the use of sudden and deadly force by a victim. On appeal, B's conviction of Voluntary Manslaughter would be **reversed and remanded** for further proceedings (a retrial) based upon the prejudicial error of the trial court Judge in instructing the jury. Finally, B's conviction of simple battery from the initial mutual combat fist fight would stand.

Scenario Fourteen
Defense of Others
No Duty to Retreat

Facts: A, 30s, and his girlfriend Y, 20s, were walking in a dangerous neighborhood along a sidewalk at night. A lowered 1942 Chevrolet drives by with four gang-bangers inside and loud rap music booming. Moments later, two men, B and C, both in their 20s, wearing gang clothing and with gang tattoos, suddenly emerge from a nearby alley and confront A and Y. B and C both pull blades and threaten to rape Y and kill A. B flashes a gang sign to C. Unable to retreat because of the danger to Y, A disarms and kills B with B's knife. C takes off running. A pursues C for a half of a block and engages him. C attempts to use his knife against A, but A kills C with B's knife. Police are called by local residents, and multiple witnesses describe the facts and also report the threatening statements by B and C. However, one witness informs the police that C was trying to get away, had given up the fight and was killed,

Stand Your Ground—
TO KILL, OR NOT TO KILL...

"...without no just cause, you know what I mean? I mean, the dude had given up the fight and was just tryin' to get away!"

A admits that C ran off when A disarmed and killed B, but informs the police that he feared that C would get nearby gang reinforcements to immediately return to kill A and rape and kill Y on the spot. Also, A points out that when he was running, A was always in close proximity to C. A explains further that when he caught C, C tried to use C's knife against him. A is arrested for and charged with the murder of C.

Analysis: While A and Y may not have been wise to walk at night in such a dangerous neighborhood, they had no duty to pick a different route or activity. When the two men confront them, pull knives and threaten to rape Y and kill A, A obviously has the right to use deadly force to defend himself and Y from these deadly force assailants/felony perpetrators. A reasonable person in A's circumstance would believe that the use of deadly force would be necessary to repel the unlawful attack. Moreover, A would certainly be justified in not retreating, even if there were a duty to retreat, since that could further endanger Y. When A disarms B and uses B's knife to kill B, this use of deadly force is reasonable under the circumstances and constitutes the lawful and justifiable use of deadly

Scenario Fourteen

force. However, at that point C takes off running. **Was A's pursuit and killing of C justified as self-defense and the defense of another (Y)?**

Where a defense to an attack is so successful that the attacker is rendered **incapable** of inflicting further injury, or if by virtue of any other circumstance the danger **no longer exists**, there is no legal justification for further attack, punishment, revenge or retaliation. In *Maurer v. State* (Ind. 1891) 29 N.E. 392, 129 Ind. 587, the assailant was 7 feet away, had discarded his weapon and was turning away at the time defendant assaulted him. The Court held,

> "One cannot, after his enemy has cast away his weapon, and turned to fly, kill him, and successfully claim to have been acting in self-defense." (29 NE at 393)

In *Com. v. Daniels* (Pa. 1973) 302 A.2d 841, 451 Pa. 163 defendant had been tried for the murder of one man and assault with a deadly weapon of a second man in one incident. There, four men came to the door of defendant's residence and when defendant opened the door, man number One demanded, in a threatening manner, payment of a debt. Defendant kicked One down a flight of stairs, but One started up the stairs with "something like brass knuckles... with a fork sticking out." Defendant met One halfway, pulled a knife and stabbed him, killing him. *Daniels* reversed the murder conviction as to victim One, holding that defendant's conduct in stabbing him was

Stand Your Ground—
TO KILL, OR NOT TO KILL...

justifiable self-defense. However, after such stabbing in self-defense, defendant ascended the stairway and confronted man number Two, stabbing him in the chest. **Defendant thereupon pursued Two down the hallway and stabbed him *again*, this time in the back.** Defendant's conviction for assault with a deadly weapon against Two was upheld in *Daniels*, since that attack was not deemed to have been in self-defense.

In *People v. Keys* (1944) 62 Cal.App.2d 903, 916, 145 P.2d 589, a defendant in a gunfight was not protected by a claim of self-defense where defendant shot the fatal shot at the victim's **back** after the victim had abandoned the conflict and started running away. Similarly, in *People v. Tamkin* (1882) 62 Cal. 468 the Court held that self-defense in a gunshot killing had **not** been established when the victim, after using profanity and threats, turned and walked away before being shot. In *People v. Evans* (1969) 2 Cal.App.3d 877, 882, 82 Cal.Rptr. 877, the Court held that the right of self-defense **ended** when a defendant brandished a knife and commenced chasing after an unarmed person. In *People v. Conkling* (1896) 111 Cal. 616, 44 P. 314, the California Supreme Court advised that where the danger had ceased,

> "Killing under such circumstances is not done in self-defense, for the necessity to kill is not present, but is simply wreaking vengeance in satisfaction of a prior wrong." (111 Cal. at 626)

Nevertheless, as held in *People v. Hatchett* (1942)

Scenario Fourteen

56 Cal.App.2d 20, 22, 132 P.2d 51, the "stand his ground" doctrine bestows upon a defendant **an important corollary aspect of self-defense**: If the fleeing attacker **still represents a realistic threat of serious bodily injury or death**, a defendant may **pursue** the attacker until that defendant has made himself safe from danger. The California Supreme Court in *People v. Hecker (1895) 109 Cal. 451, 42 P. 307* cautioned that,

> "[T]he pursuit must not be in revenge, nor after the necessity for defense has ceased, but must be prosecuted in good faith to the sole end of winning his safety and securing his life." (109 Cal. at 463)

In the present scenario, B and C wore gang-affiliated clothing and were both heavily tatted, and gang signs were flashed in the course of the assault on A and Y. After A killed B, C ran off but did **not** appear to discard his knife. A subjectively believed that C was a gang-member and would recruit other nearby gang members to attack and kill A and to rape and kill Y. Based upon these beliefs, and in the heat of the moment having just disarmed and killed B, A pursued and caught up to C a half block away, whereupon C attempted to use C's knife against A. A then killed C. A witness complained to police that there was "no just cause" for A's killing C, since C was "just tryin' to get away." Although this is a close call, A would likely be entitled to a jury instruction as to self-defense and pursuit of an attacker until

Stand Your Ground —
TO KILL, OR NOT TO KILL...

the threat has been neutralized. At trial, the defense argument would be strong that the attack by B and C was probably gang-related (neighborhood, tattoos, gang-style clothing, gang-hand signs) and a reasonable person in A's circumstances could reasonably fear that C would recruit other nearby gang members and return promptly to kill A and kill or rape Y. However, a prosecuting attorney might argue to the contrary that the danger had passed when C ran off and that any fear of gang-member reinforcements was **pure speculation**. Most jury members, in my opinion, would not split hairs on this issue and would vote that A's actions, of quickly pursuing and overtaking C and killing C when C again used his knife against A, constituted a **justifiable** use of force in self-defense and the defense of others.

Even in a duty to retreat jurisdiction, the whole point behind A's pursuit of C as C ran away was that there was **no completely safe retreat possible** there, where A and Y had no vehicle and found themselves a likely target in a gang neighborhood with an immediately recent attack and killing of a gang member. Had C been able to recruit reinforcements, A and Y could have been easily overwhelmed by superior numbers of assailants. This does not appear to be a case where A's killing of C was of wreaking **vengeance** in satisfaction of a prior wrong, after the necessity for defense had ceased. This was a case where A reasonably believed that he needed to stop C from securing gang reinforcements that would quickly

Scenario Fourteen

return to physically harm A and Y. Accordingly, A's act of pursuing and killing C with B's knife would probably be found to be legally justified as both self-defense and the defense of others to protect Y from death or serious bodily injury (rape).

Stand Your Ground—
TO KILL, OR NOT TO KILL...

Scenario Fifteen
Imminent Harm

Facts: A, a 17 year old high school senior of slight build, but studying martial arts, has long been the subject of ridicule by B, also a high school senior and of substantially larger physical stature than A. For weeks, B has repeatedly threatened A that on the day after Graduation, several months away, B intends to ambush A and beat him up. A tells his martial arts instructor about the threats and works on his rear-leg front thrust kick for a couple of weeks. Thereafter, B again threatens that on the day after Graduation, still several months away, B is going to beat A up. A is in actual fear of being ambushed by B and beaten up, and so after school, A walks up to B in the school courtyard and kicks B in the stomach with a rear-leg front thrust kick. As B is doubled over, laying on his side gasping for air, A advises B, "Don't ever threaten me again. Next time, it won't be so easy!" School officials detain both boys. B admits threatening A repeatedly and

Scenario Fifteen

confirms that he intended to beat up A, but not until the day after Graduation so that it would not affect B's Graduation. A admits to kicking B but explains that A was afraid that if he didn't stop B from threatening him, B would hurt him severely on the day after Graduation. A is arrested and charged, in Juvenile Court, with the Juvenile Court equivalent of Battery.

Analysis: This unfortunate situation is only too common as to persistent and credible threats by one student, the bully, against another student, the victim. However, instead of reporting the incidents to his parents and school officials, A sought only to improve his martial arts skills and his confidence to inflict harm. Being trained in the fighting arts is a good thing if done for the **right purpose**: to have these skills available for use if the unlawful harm is ***imminent***. Here, A developed his rear-leg front thrust kick to such a level that he was able to hurt B and possibly to dissuade B from further threats or from any attack on A.

However, A's karate kick to B's stomach was lawful **only if the peril threatened by B was *"imminent."*** As ruled by a California Court of Appeal in *People v. Hill* (2005) 131 Cal.App.4th 1089, 31 Cal.Rptr. 891, a

> "[f]ear of future harm—no matter how great the fear and no matter how great the likelihood of the harm—will not suffice [for perfect or imperfect self-defense]." (131 Cal.App.4th at 1101)

Stand Your Ground—
TO KILL, OR NOT TO KILL...

In *People v. Aris* (1989) 215 Cal.App.3d 1178, 264 Cal.Rptr. 167, the trial Judge had instructed the jury that,

> "'imminent peril,' as used in these [jury] instructions, means that the peril must have existed or appeared to the defendant to have existed at **the very time the fatal shot was fired**. In other words, the peril must appear to the defendant as immediate and present and not prospective or even in the near future. An imminent peril is one that, from appearances, **must be instantly dealt with**." (bold added for emphasis)

The Court of Appeal in *Aris* held that the foregoing jury instruction was correct. (215 Cal.App.3d at 1187). Accord, *In re Christian S*. (1994) 7 Cal.4th 768, 783, 30 Cal.Rptr. 33, 872 P.2d 574.

In *State v. Wilson* (Wash. 1894) 39 P. 106, 10 Wash. 402, the Washington Supreme Court considered an appeal by defendant ("appellant") of the denial of a motion for a new trial following his conviction of Murder in the Second Degree. In *Wilson*, defendant had walked with the victim away from defendant's home, trying to get the victim to stay away from defendant's sister, who was also the victim's wife, and to not communicate further with her. The victim vacillated between saying he would stay away, return and harm her or force her to leave defendant's home with the victim (her husband). Finally, about a mile

Scenario Fifteen

away from the residence, the victim turned around and headed back, declaring that he would kill his wife and then himself. Defendant knew that the victim carried a loaded revolver, but he also knew that defendant's father was at the home, that the father possessed two firearms at the home and that the father would attempt to protect the father's daughter (victim's wife) from harm. Under these circumstances (according to defendant's version of the evidence), defendant chose to pick up a heavy stick and crush the victim's skull, killing him. The Court wrote,

> "...[T]hereupon appellant picked up a stick and struck him a single blow, which killed him...The facts proven in connection with the autopsy of the body show that a blow of such violence had been received by the deceased as to crush in the entire back portion of the head and dislocate the neck." (39 P. at 107)

The Court held on appeal that the defense of the defense of others was not proved,

> "His theory is that he was justified in what he did, upon the ground that it was in defense of his sister. But we are unable to hold that his sister was shown to be **in such imminent danger** as to justify the taking of life." (39 P. at 107) (bold added for emphasis)

The Court explained further,

> "It appeared that the deceased had been

Stand Your Ground —
TO KILL, OR NOT TO KILL...

in the habit of threatening his wife, whenever he lost his temper, to such an extent that such threats did not make it probable that she would be injured; much less did it make the injury so imminent as to justify such extreme measures for her protection." (39 P. at 108)

Wilson held that the denial of defendant's motion for a new trial was proper. Accordingly, the conviction of Murder was upheld on appeal.

In the instant Scenario, the future harm to A was objectively very likely and very substantial. B had both the apparent ability and the repeatedly expressed intent of finding A and beating him up on the day after Graduation. B had a **size** advantage and the **strategic** advantage of picking the time and place for A's day-after-Graduation whooping. The anxiety which this caused A was no laughing matter and had to be dealt with, in some fashion. However, the peril to A was still months away. A had several reasonable alternatives, in that period of time, to the **immediate** use of force to protect himself from the future harm. Accordingly, the future harm was not, in a legal sense, "imminent." A could not lawfully act now to prevent harm that was to occur, if at all, in the **non-immediate future**. This issue should have been resolved by a combination of school administrative intervention and continued martial arts training. Also, A could have tried to avoid B following Graduation or simply have enlisted the protection of his parents or some of A's friends to deter

Scenario Fifteen

B's prospective misconduct.

In any event, the allegation of battery in this Scenario would be found to be "True" [the Juvenile Court equivalent of "Guilty"] in the Juvenile Court. Once Juvenile Court jurisdiction over A attaches, the Court could make appropriate orders within the jurisdiction of the Juvenile Court, such as for probation, community service, counseling and even confinement in a Juvenile lock-down facility (although confinement for a first offense of battery would be **very** unlikely). B could, and should, be suspended from school for an appropriate period of time for what amount to multiple terrorist threats against A.

Stand Your Ground —
TO KILL, OR NOT TO KILL...

Scenario Sixteen
Sudden and Deadly Counterassault Duty to Retreat

Facts: One day just after normal office hours at work, A, a physically capable man in his 60s, walks in the parking lot to his vehicle carrying a book **and opens the driver's door**. Just then, a co-worker, B, a physically capable man in his 50s, walks nearby heading toward his own vehicle. A walks a few feet toward B and accuses him of reporting A to their supervisor, Y, for A using company computers for personal use. B tells A, "Leave me alone, I'm just doing my job." When B tries to walk past A towards B's car, A grabs B's shoulder and hits B in the face, knocking B to the ground. B gets up, **pulls out a previously concealed locking blade combat knife**, and lunges at A, attempting to cut A's throat. A avoids B's assault, pulls his **own** combat knife and stabs B **one time** in the stomach. While B is on the pavement bleeding profusely, A dials 9-1-1 to report the incident. When police and Paramedics arrive, B is pronounced dead

Scenario Sixteen

from the stabbing wound to his abdomen. Police recover B's open knife which was lying on the ground next to B. A turns over his own knife to police. A accurately describes to a police Detective exactly how the events transpired and video surveillance footage confirms A's report of the sequence of events. Supervisor Y indicates to police that B had, in fact, reported A as having misused a company computer for personal use and that a company disciplinary charge against A was pending but had not yet been administratively resolved. A is arrested and tried for Voluntary Manslaughter and simple Battery.

Analysis: As seen above, a non-deadly aggressor, when met with sudden and deadly force may justifiably defend himself against the deadly attack. This is true because the initial use of deadly force (here, by B) was unlawful. *Watkins v. State* (1989) 79 Md.App. 136, 555 A.2d 1087; *Newman v. State* (2003) 156 Md. App. 20, 845 A.2d 71 (reversed on other grounds, 384 Md. 285, 863 A.2d 321). In California, CALJIC 5.54 (standard jury instructions) provides as follows:

> "The right of self-defense is only available to a person who initiated an assault, if, (1) He has done all the following: A. He has actually tried, in good faith, to refuse to continue fighting; B. He has by words or

Stand Your Ground—
TO KILL, OR NOT TO KILL...

conduct caused his opponent to be aware, as a reasonable person, that he wants to stop fighting; and C. He has by words or conduct caused his opponent to be aware, as a reasonable person, that he has stopped fighting. After he has done these three things, he has the right to self-defense if his opponent continues to fight, or (2) **If the victim of simple assault responds by launching *a sudden and deadly counterassault*, the original aggressor need not attempt to withdraw and may use reasonably necessary force in self-defense."** (bold and italics added for emphasis)

In the present scenario, A did not attempt withdraw from the fight, so part (1) of the CALJIC 5.54 jury instruction has not been satisfied. However, when B pulled the previously concealed combat knife and actually attempted to inflict lethal harm on A, the classic **sudden and deadly counterassault** against A occurred. A actually believed that his life was in danger, and a reasonable person in A's position and circumstance would very likely also have held that belief. Under these circumstances, the use by A of his own combat knife to defend himself when confronted by B, an armed and dangerous opponent, would likely be considered to constitute the exercise of reasonably necessary force.

However, a claim of self-defense is not available to a person who seeks out a quarrel with the fraudulent intent to force a deadly issue and thus to create a

Scenario Sixteen

real or apparent necessity to assault another. *People v. Garnier* (1950) 95 Cal.App.2d 480, 496, 213 P.2d 111. However, in the instant scenario, there is no factual indication that A orchestrated this physical encounter with B in order to provide an occasion for A to kill B. *See, State v. Bristol* (Wyo. 1938) 84 P.2d 757, 53 Wyo. 304, *infra* (the issue of self-defense turns on whether the accused's conduct was reasonably calculated to provoke the deceased into attacking the accused). To the contrary, the encounter appears to have been **a simple work-place dispute** resulting in a fist fight. B's combat knife was concealed prior to B pulling it and attempting to cut A's throat and there is neither an indication that B had a propensity for knife fighting nor that A believed that B would pull a knife. The fact that A was carrying a knife is of some interest, but is certainly not dispositive since carrying a folding, lockable knife is typically not illegal and is somewhat commonplace. Thus, in a no-duty-to-retreat State, A would likely be found Not Guilty of Voluntary Manslaughter since his conduct was in the exercise of lawful self-defense.

There were other, theoretically safe, options for A. A might have disarmed B, distracted B by calling out the name of the supervisor then making a run for it, thrown his book at B, kicked B in the groin and neutralized the knife threat, reasoned with B, or even cut B's arm in a non-deadly strike, causing B to drop his weapon. Although these options may be taken into account as factors in determining whether the level of

Stand Your Ground —
TO KILL, OR NOT TO KILL...

force used by A was objectively reasonable, no rule of law allows a Judge or Jury to substitute its judgment for what **means and manner** of defense is used, only whether the means of defense was objectively reasonable—**except** in a duty to retreat State.

As seen above, a **minority** of jurisdictions has adopted a **duty to retreat** rule. A "duty to retreat" law typically requires a defender to retreat prior to his use of deadly force, so long as that retreat would be "completely safe." A prosecutor in the instant Scenario could argue that A had the opportunity to effect a **completely safe retreat** into the open door of A's vehicle. *See, People v. Aiken* (N.Y. 2005) 828 N.E.2d 74, 795 N.Y.Supp.2d 158, 4 N.Y.3d 324, *infra*,

> "Here, defendant need only have closed the door, or pulled up the drawbridge, to be secure in his castle." (795 N.Y.Supp.2d at 163)

Along this line of argument, A was purportedly only a **door lock away** from safety. Thus, a life (B's life) could theoretically have been saved had A simply fled to the complete safety of his vehicle. Such a result is **much** easier said than done. A duty to retreat rule of law has **potentially *fatal shortcomings*** for the defender. The duty to retreat does not generally come into play **unless the defender is faced with imminent harm from deadly force**. In a duty to retreat State, the defender facing such imminent harm from deadly force may be **deemed** by a jury to have been actually aware of any reasonably obvious means of

Scenario Sixteen

retreat (e.g., stepping back inside an open doorway and closing the door). If a jury also determines that any such known means of retreat are "completely safe," then the **defender *must* have chosen that option** when dealing with the deadly force he is facing. Yet, there is a Catch-22. If the case is in court in a criminal prosecution, **the defender did *not* choose that option of retreat**. Had a retreat, taken by the defender, been completely safe, then the defender **would not be a defendant in a criminal prosecution**! In order for a prosecution of the defender to exist, the defender did not actually know of the completely safe retreat or chose not to risk retreat and instead, simply defended himself.

A duty to retreat rule of law eventually puts a jury in the untenable position of deciding the **appropriate *means* of defense**—not whether the selected level of force (e.g., deadly force) is reasonable, but **whether the defendant's choice of *means* of defense is the most desirable**. Without having been in the line of fire, without having experienced the adrenalin rush of the heat of battle, without having had one's **life literally on the line**, a jury will be required to **substitute its collective judgment** for that of the defender as to whether a "completely safe" retreat was reasonably known and available to the defender. In a duty to retreat State, a defender in a real-time, life and death crisis is placed in the impossible, seemingly contradictory, position of (knowing this duty to retreat law exists in the particular State in which he finds

Stand Your Ground —
TO KILL, OR NOT TO KILL...

himself and) **looking for a way to retreat** before responding to **imminent harm** of deadly force. To require this of a defender is, in practice, **impossibly obscure, unpredictable, unreliable, unjust and counter-intuitive** to the notion of allowing a defender reasonable latitude in self-defense.

The most likely, and most socially desirable, outcome for A in a duty to retreat State would be that a jury would find that an attempted retreat into A's vehicle would have been unreasonably risky and thus **not** a "completely safe" retreat. A's self-defense claim to Voluntary Manslaughter would be successful. From the outset, however, A could be convicted of simple battery, since grabbing and punching B was an act of unprovoked aggression and was not in the exercise of any colorable self-defense.

Scenario Seventeen
Imminent Harm
Reasonable Belief

Facts: A is crossing the street in a crosswalk when a hot-headed motorist, B, yells from a car for A to "Speed it up." B continues to speak menacingly to A, telling A, "You punk, I'll get outta this car and beat your ass." B does get out of the car, hands and arms up and out to the side, speaking in an excited speech pattern with some slurred words. B has what appear to be jailhouse tattoos on his arms and neck. A warns B, "Stay away from me. I don't want any trouble from you. Stay away!" B continues to slowly but deliberately close the distance, and when B is approximately eight feet away from A, B turns his head away momentarily. At this time, A rushes forward and rear-leg roundhouse kicks B to the stomach. A punches B in the face, foot sweeps B to the ground and hits B in the face again before B loses consciousness. A police car pulls up and when B comes to, B requests that the police arrest A for battery. A bystander's smart-phone video picked up

Stand Your Ground—
TO KILL, OR NOT TO KILL...

the full audio/video of this encounter. In a citizen's arrest undertaken by police at B's request, A is arrested for and charged with battery.

Analysis: Importantly, a person is not required to allow an assailant to **strike first** in order to justify the use of otherwise appropriate force in self-defense. As ruled in *People v. Adams* (2007) 176 Cal.App.4th 946, 98 Cal.Rptr.3d 383,

> "If the arresting party swings a fist, the arrestee need not suffer the blow before undertaking to defend himself."

When a rifle was aimed at defendant, **he need not wait to see** if the decedent's rifle could shoot before acting on reasonable appearances and taking reasonable measures of self-defense. *Cox v. State* (Ala. App. 1923) 96 So. 83, 19 Ala.App. 205. *See also, State v. Matthews* (Mo. 1899) 49 S.W. 1085, 148 Mo. 185; *State v. McGee* (Mo. 1950) 234 S.W.2d 587, 361 Mo. 309; *State v. Connally* (Or. Cir. 1869) 3 Or. 69, *infra*. If the rule were otherwise, a person about to be attacked might never have the opportunity to defend himself, if rendered helpless by an aggressor's first strike.

However, as we have seen, a defender's subjective belief in the need to apply reasonable force in response to a perceived imminent harm, must of course be **objectively reasonable**. From an interior

Scenario Seventeen

landing outside his 2nd floor apartment, defendant observed the front door to the apartment complex rattling at the bottom of the stairway. Defendant got his gun and, believing that a burglar was breaking into the apartment house, fired two shots in the direction of the front door, killing...the milkman. The Court in *Com. v. Harris* (Pa. 1971) 281 A.2d 879, 444 Pa. 515 held that where no entry to the apartment house had been made and the front door was not shaking, the belief that a burglar was attempting to enter the apartments was, as a matter of law, not reasonable and thus the killing could not be justified by the defense of self-defense.

In the instant case, **experts would testify** that everything about B's conduct indicated both his **intent** to attack A and the **imminence** of the attack. Looking away is often a tactic of aggressors intending to launch a surprise attack. Hands up and out are known by experts to be an attempt to intimidate an intended victim. An excited speech pattern with some slurred words may likely indicate a high level of adrenalin in the attacker. B was closing the distance on A despite A's **harsh admonitions** for B to stay back. B's verbal threats were real, and perceived as real, and B was clearly only a split-second away from physically attacking A. Under these circumstances, A was fully justified in the use of non-deadly force to repel this imminent attack, **even before** B actually threw any punch at A.

Stand Your Ground—
TO KILL, OR NOT TO KILL...

Moreover, the force used by A was not "deadly" force, since it was not likely to cause death or great bodily injury. As noted above, great bodily injury is, "a significant or substantial physical injury" (California Penal Code Sect. 198.5) or an injury that results in serious disfigurement, loss of any member or organ of the body or a permanent prolonged impairment of the use of any member or organ of the body [*Shorter v. People* (1849) 2 N.Y. 193, 51 Am. Dec. 286]. In the instant scenario, A simply worked B over with non-lethal self-defense methods until B was unconscious, and then A stopped.
The facts were borne out by A's testimony and the video surveillance evidence. A is free and clear of wrongdoing. Moreover, A could successfully sue B civilly for false arrest and collect damages for pain and suffering and damage to his reputation in the community as a law-abiding citizen.

Scenario Eighteen
Excessive Force by a Peace Officer

Facts: A, an ex-felon in possession of a concealed firearm on his person, is stopped while driving by a City police officer, B, for a no tail light violation. As an ex-felon, A is forbidden by law from owning or possessing a concealable firearm. On B's police vehicle computer screen, B learns that A is an ex-felon, previously convicted of felony battery with great bodily injury against a police officer (for which he served a prison sentence), and that A is also subject to arrest on a misdemeanor Warrant for Failure to Appear (a misdemeanor or infraction) on a speeding ticket. B turns off his patrol-vehicle video recorder. B then informs A that he is under arrest for a misdemeanor Failure to Appear Warrant, and orders A out of the vehicle. B orders A to prone-out on the ground with his arms and legs outstretched. When A complies, B extracts his baton from its holder at B's side and proceeds to **beat A severely to the body and head** with

Stand Your Ground—
TO KILL, OR NOT TO KILL...

the baton. Believing his life to be in danger, A extracts a **concealed gun** from his ankle holster and shoots police officer B, killing him. A is later arrested, and upon physical exam at the jail, multiple baton-strike bruises on his body and two deep lacerations to his face and skull are documented and photographed. The District Attorney charges A with possession of a firearm by a person previously convicted of a felony and for Murder of a police officer, and seeks the death penalty against A for the Murder. A files a civil lawsuit against the City for personal injuries resulting from B's use of excessive force against him.

Analysis: While ex-felons may be prohibited from possessing a concealable firearm (e.g., California Penal Code Sect. 12021), **ex-felons do not give up all rights to use force in self-defense**. A defendant who was in unlawful possession of a weapon at the time of shooting another may still claim and prove self-defense if the defendant was in any event entitled to arm himself for purposes of self-defense at the time of the shooting. State v. Burriss (S.C. 1999) 513 S.E.2d 104, 334 S.C. 256.

A correctional officer may not use unreasonable or excessive force while escorting an inmate. If the officer does use such excessive or unreasonable force, the prisoner may lawfully defend himself against such unlawful use of force. People v. Coleman (1978) 84 Cal.

Scenario Eighteen

App.3d 1016, 1022, 149 Cal.Rptr. 134.

In *Copeland v. State* (1846) 26 Tenn. 479, 7 Hum. 394, defendant, Mary Copeland, was going her own road in a laudable pursuit on the way to church and was assailed in that road by Ruth, a romantic rival armed with a hickory stick of a dangerous character. On appeal following her conviction of Murder, the Court held that when defendant then and there slew her adversary with a knife, the homicide was not murder and instead was legally justified as self-defense, or at most Manslaughter. *Copeland v. State* (Tenn. 1846) 26 Tenn. 394, 408, 7 Hum. 479.

Also, an ex-felon may use a concealable firearm in lawful self-defense. Statutes prohibiting possession of a concealable firearm by an ex-felon are not intended to preclude the use of such firearms in self-defense by an ex-felon. The Court in *People v. King* (1978) 22 Cal.3d 12, 23, 148 Cal.Rptr. 409, 582 P.2d 1000 held that denying ex-felons the right to use a concealable weapon in self-defense, when they continue to have the right to use even deadlier non-concealable weapons for this purpose, would lead to absurd results. In *State v. Bowling* (Tenn. 1880) 3 Tenn.Cas. 110, 3 Shan. 110, when defendant was confronted with a threat of imminent deadly force, defendant defended himself with an unlawfully concealed weapon. *Bowling* held that carrying an unlawfully concealed weapon does not strip the defendant of the right to use such weapon in appropriate circumstances in self-defense.

Stand Your Ground—
TO KILL, OR NOT TO KILL...

In the present case, the police officer, B, was in the process of effectuating a lawful arrest of A on the misdemeanor Warrant for a Failure to Appear in court on a traffic infraction. B became aware of A's prior felony conviction for battery on a peace officer with great bodily injury. At that point, B would certainly have been within his right to order A to prone out in the beginning stages of what is known as a "felony stop" procedure. B could have called for back-up, or could have handcuffed A himself, though A was presenting no overt threat to B. Importantly, however, A was not in any manner acting in such a way as to justify B striking him at all, or repeatedly, with a baton.

A police baton is a dangerous and deadly weapon, banned from possession by non-police persons except in the context of certain limited martial arts training. As B beat A to the head and body with the baton, A actually and reasonably believed that his life was in

---

[21] "Imperfect" self-defense is not a true defense, but is more in the nature of an aspect of Voluntary Manslaughter. *People v. Barton* (1995) 12 Cal.4th 186, 199, 47 Cal.Rptr. 569, 906 P.2d 531. Imperfect self-defense occurs when a defendant has an actual, **but unreasonable**, belief that he (or, in the case of defense of others, someone he seeks to protect) is being subjected to unlawful force, and then the defendant uses force which, if the belief were reasonable, would be reasonably necessary. For example, in *People v. Blakely* (2000) 23 Cal.4th 82, 91, 96 Cal.Rptr.2d 451, 999 P.2d 675, the Court described that imperfect self-defense would result in a reduction of a murder charge to Voluntary Manslaughter where a defendant, with an intent to kill or with conscious disregard for life, unlawfully kills in an **unreasonable** belief in the need for self-defense.

Scenario Eighteen

danger. When A elected to pull the concealed firearm to overcome B's excessive deadly force, he acted in what is known as "perfect" self-defense[21] and his killing of B was justifiable. Any prosecution of A for Murder or even for Voluntary Manslaughter would result in a Not Guilty verdict or a Directed Verdict of Not Guilty. A would, however, be found Guilty of a violation of the felony prohibition against an ex-felon possessing a concealable firearm. A could successfully sue the City in a civil lawsuit for personal injuries suffered as a result of B's application of excessive force by the use of his baton.

Stand Your Ground—
TO KILL, OR NOT TO KILL...

Scenario Nineteen
Alcohol and Mental Illness

Facts: A, a 250 pound schizophrenic alcoholic, is sitting in a corner of a park during the daytime. A just finished polishing off a gallon of red wine consumed over a period of an hour or so. A lone dark cloud drifts over the entire park, followed by a brisk breeze. A begins to "hear" voices (auditory hallucinations) convincing him that the world is quickly coming to an end and that evil extraterrestrials from another universe have invaded the earth. The voices tell A that the extraterrestrials will look like humans and will **come *after him* because A is the *only hope* for the survival of human civilization.** If he stops the extraterrestials, the voices say, he will save the earth from destruction. Two women, B and C, are jogging together through the park in his general direction. A gets up from his corner and stumbles toward the path on which B and C are running. Seeing A's approach, B yells out to A, "Hey, stay away!" C, a *Martial Arts for Christian Values* national association

Scenario Nineteen

member, slows, extracts a **heavy cross** from her backpack and walks toward A. C tells A, "Here, stop. I'll minister to you." Because of the influence of alcohol, A thinks C just said, "There's no cops. I'll murder you." Believing that C is about to assault him with the cross, A picks up a large rock and hits C in the head, killing her instantly. A yells out to B in slurred speech,

> "Satan sent you from the stars. But I'm the last hope, the last hope. You're the evil ones up there with your staffs of iron and I'll kill you all!"

Soon, local police arrive and A, volunteers,

> "All the cops are dead, the cops are dead! She told me, 'There's no cops, so I'll murder you, murder you.' But I saved the earth. It was **me!**"

B informs the police that actually, as C approached A, C stated to A, "Here, stop. I'll minister to you", not "I'll murder you." A is arrested and charged with murder.

Analysis: C was a Good Samaritan who believed that she could help the intoxicated A by proselytizing her religion to him. She slowed her run and approached A, extracting a heavy cross from her backpack that she often carried for just such an

Stand Your Ground—
TO KILL, OR NOT TO KILL...

occasion. Believing that she could turn a chronically alcoholic homeless man into a Christian by her words and caring nature, C stated to A, "Here, stop, I'll minister to you." Piecing together the evidence, A most likely **misunderstood** C's words because of his consumption of **excessive quantities of alcohol**. A subjectively believed that C was approaching him, with a heavy "staff of iron" in her hand. Moreover, because of A's paranoid schizophrenia, A believed that he was hearing special communications (the voices) to him instructing that he was to be the **savior of the world** against evil extraterrestrial intruders. Saving the world was, he believed, his personal **manifest destiny**. While the schizophrenia may be the basis for a Not Guilty by Reason of Insanity defense (and if successful, resulting in involuntary confinement for an indefinite period of time in a mental institution), neither alcohol nor mental illness can serve to make the **unlawful** use of force lawful as "perfect" self-defense.

In a murder prosecution, the defendant was not entitled to have the jury consider his level of intoxication as a factor in determining the objective reasonableness of his subjective belief of the need to use deadly force at the time of his stabbing of the deceased. The test is not what a reasonably prudent **intoxicated** person would believe as to the need for self-defense. The test is what a **reasonably prudent person would perceive**. *State v. Brown* (Conn.App. 1990) 577 A.2d 1120, 22 Conn.App. 521. In *Springfield v. State* (1892) 96 Ala. 81, 11 So. 250, the

Scenario Nineteen

Court held that a person who because of voluntary intoxication thinks that he is in danger of imminent attack, though a sober man would not have thought so, does not have the "reasonable" belief which the law requires for a claim of self-defense.

In *People v. Mejia-Lenares* (2006) 135 Cal.App.4th 1437, 38 Cal.Rptr.3d 404, a California Court of Appeal held that the trial court's ruling that **imperfect** self-defense had not been established was proper and not in error. In *Mejia-Lenares*, defendant had fatally stabbed the victim out of fear that the victim was **transforming into the devil** and wanted to kill defendant. Despite conceding that defendant had imagined the victim's ignominious transformation, defendant presented evidence that at or near the time of the homicide, defendant was diagnosed with major depression having psychotic dimensions, including **delusions**. The trial court ruled that while evidence of delusions may have been relevant in a jury's determination of the **degree of murder**, it would *not* be proper in a jury's consideration of whether imperfect self-defense was established by the defendant as an affirmative defense to murder. The Court wrote that imperfect self-defense is "a species of mistake of fact…; as such, it cannot be founded on delusion," which is a concept far afield from fact or reason. The Court explained further that,

"[A] mistake of fact is predicated upon a negligent perception of facts, not, as in the

Stand Your Ground—
TO KILL, OR NOT TO KILL...

case of a delusion, a perception of facts **not grounded in reality**." (135 Cal.App.4th at 1453; bold added for emphasis)

In the present case, absent A's alcohol intoxication, he would likely have heard and understood C's **actual**, innocuous, words. Moreover, although A's mental illness may have assisted A in a plea of Not Guilty by Reason of Insanity, it would not assist A in defending against the murder charge with either perfect or imperfect self-defense. To a **reasonable** (sober and non-schizophrenic) observer from A's perspective, C's intent and actions were **only** consistent with a peaceable, albeit arguably misguided, attempt to guide A out of alcohol abuse and into the loving hands of C's subjective notion of religion. Accordingly, no successful claim to perfect self-defense could be made by A. Also, since delusions are by definition not grounded in reality, A will be unable to successfully have the charges reduced, by the jury, to Voluntary Manslaughter on the basis of an assertion of imperfect self-defense.

Scenario Twenty
Transferred Intent

Facts: A, a capable man in his 50s, drives into a Post Office parking lot just as B, a disgruntled and mentally unstable husband/father in his 40s (going through a messy divorce and child custody battle), is in the process of shooting and killing multiple people, including B's wife, Y, inside the Post Office. A enters the Post office as B is attempting to flee the scene with gun in hand. A sees the melee and attempts to disarm B. In the struggle, A deliberately discharges B's gun (trying to shoot B) but instead hits a postal clerk, X, killing him. A pulls the trigger a second time, this time hitting and killing the intended target, B. When police arrive, A is arrested for and later charged with Voluntary Manslaughter for the shooting of X. X's widow files a civil suit against A for Wrongful Death.

Analysis: Here, A happens upon a horrendous crime spree in progress, with Y and several other

Stand Your Ground—
TO KILL, OR NOT TO KILL...

persons dead or dying at the scene inside the Post Office. The fact that B may be in the process of leaving the immediate scene of the mass murders does not mean that the threat of imminent harm has passed. Virtually **anything** was still possible from B in this situation, including B shooting A on the way out the door, B killing innocent bystanders/witnesses outside the Post Office premises, B taking a hostage, B shooting at police, or even B returning to the Post Office to kill more victims there. A rightly disarms B and attempts with deadly force (B's gun) to kill B. However, when A shoots at B, he instead hits and kills the postal clerk, X. **Since X might not have been killed had A not intervened, is A guilty of Voluntary Manslaughter?**

The defense of self-defense, and of defense of others, is not lost when a person who attempts to batter or kill an aggressor inadvertently hits a bystander. By virtue of the doctrine of "transferred intent," the **absence** of criminal intent toward the aggressor is "transferred," as a matter of law, to the unintended victim. *People v. Matthews* (1979) 91 Cal. App.3d 1019, 1024, 154 Cal.Rptr. 628; *People v. Levitt* (1984) 156 Cal.App.3d 500, 507, 203 Cal.Rptr. 276; 55 ALR3d 620 [unintended killing of or injury to a bystander during attempted self-defense]. The doctrine operates to excuse a battery upon an unintended victim. *V.M. v. State* (Fla. Dist. Ct. App. 4th Dist. 2000) 766 So.2d 280. The accidental killing of a bystander by the defendant who was acting in self-defense

Scenario Twenty

constitutes a justifiable homicide. *State v. Labbee* (Wash. 1925) 234 P. 1049, 134 Wash. 55.

In the present case, A intended to kill B in order to halt B's murder spree. The unintended killing of X, while highly unfortunate, would be considered, under the doctrine of transferred intent, to constitute a justifiable homicide in the lawful exercise of force in defense of others (and in self-defense, as well). The Voluntary Manslaughter charge would be dismissed by the Court and the civil suit against A filed by X's widow would likewise fail.

Stand Your Ground —
TO KILL, OR NOT TO KILL...

CONCLUDING OBSERVATIONS

Outside of the martial arts studio, fighting techniques and weapons skills are for use in real-life situations as a **last resort** in the face of an imminent threat of harm. If faced with such harm, one should of course defend oneself and others whose safety is threatened. One may, however, suffer **substantial adverse legal consequences, civilly or through the criminal justice system**, unless a reasonable person in the same or similar circumstances would have acted similarly. The reasonable person must have believed that force was necessary to avert the unlawful threat of imminent harm and also that the force actually used was itself reasonably necessary to avert that harm. Complicating matters is the fact that in a minority of jurisdictions, a **duty to retreat** will allow a jury to second-guess a defender's decision to act with deadly force—that is, to substitute its own judgment as to whether a **completely safe retreat**, known to the defender but not taken, was accessible. And even then, there is the impact of the X-factor discussed above where an unfair and unjust result, not based in actual

Concluding Observations

fact, may result in the system of justice whenever force is used by one person against another.

The bottom line is that the **legal limits of safety** are based in both fact and law. While an **aggressor** may have a **single-purpose focus** of harming you, a loved one or even a stranger in your presence, **you** must not lose sight of the **framework of laws pertaining to lawful defensive conduct.** View dangerous circumstances as dispassionately as feasible under the circumstances. Allow adrenaline to bolster your confidence to act with a calm but purposeful manner. Be mindful of your environment. Consider retreating if a means of retreat is clearly accessible and completely safe. Refrain from escalating a fist fight into the application of deadly force, but understand that a jury will not nicely gauge, with detached reflection, your level of force in defense so long as it is grounded in necessity. Stop when your assailant is defenseless. Promptly seek official law enforcement intervention.

So, the next time your martial arts instructor advises you to have "situational awareness," take that advice seriously and act accordingly and reasonably. In other words, always strive to make your self-defense, defense of property and defense of others both **physically effective and legally justified**.

Stand Your Ground—
TO KILL, OR NOT TO KILL...

APPENDIX

The Maryland Supreme Court, in *Sydnor v. State* (2001) 776 A.2d 669, 673-674, 365 Md. 205, 211-215, offers a **compelling compendium of English common law** pertaining to the use of force in a defense based on necessity. The *Sydnor* Court wrote:

"The **right to act in self-defense** has been regarded as a natural right, taken all but for granted, but, as a legal defense to a charge of homicide, it **was not part of early English common law**.... [F]rom the beginning of the jurisdiction of the king's courts over crime to the reign of Edward I in the Thirteenth Century, homicide could be justified only when committed in execution of the king's writ or, by custom, when apprehending an outlaw who resisted.... The privilege to use deadly force in self-defense developed from two strains of English law. Blackstone, citing both Hawkins and Hale, observed that there were three kinds of homicide— justifiable, excusable, and felonious. WILLIAM BLACKSTONE, 4 COMMENTARIES ON THE LAWS OF ENGLAND 177 (1769). **Justifiable** homicide was one 'owing to some unavoidable *necessity*, without any will, intention, or desire, and without any inadvertence or negligence, in the party killing, and therefore

Appendix

without any shadow of blame.' *Id.* at 178. It was a homicide committed by the absolute command of the law, either for the advancement of public justice (as where a public officer kills in the execution of his or her office) or for the prevention of some atrocious crime which could not otherwise be avoided. *Id.* at 179-80. As to the latter, Blackstone noted, as an example, that '[i]f any person attempts a robbery or murder of another, or attempts to break open a house **in the night time**, (which extends also to an attempt to burn it,) and shall be killed in such attempt, the slayer shall be acquitted and discharged.' Id. at 180. 'This reaches,' he continued, 'not to any crime unaccompanied with force, as picking of pockets; or to the breaking open of any house *in the day time*, unless it carries with it an attempt of robbery also.' *Id.* In the case of a justifiable homicide, Blackstone stated, the slayer was entirely without fault and was entitled to acquittal. No duty to retreat, in an effort to avoid the need to use deadly force, attended a justifiable homicide. An **excusable** homicide, according to Blackstone, could be of two types—*per infortunium*, or misadventure, and *se defendendo*, or self-defense. The first was where one doing a lawful act, without any intention to harm, unfortunately killed another, as where the head of a hatchet being lawfully used by a person flew off and killed a bystander. The second type, he made clear, was distinguishable from the justifiable variety of homicide 'calculated to hinder the perpetration of a capital crime' and concerned the case of a person protecting himself or herself

Stand Your Ground —
TO KILL, OR NOT TO KILL...

'from an assault, or the like, in the course of a sudden brawl or quarrel, by killing him who assaults him.' *Id.* at 183-84. In that situation, which the writers of the time called *chance-medley*, the right of natural defense did not include attacking the assailant, and, to excuse homicide by a plea of self-defense, 'it must appear that the slayer had no other possible means of escaping from his assailant.' *Id.* at 184. Thus, 'the law requires, that the person, who kills another in his own defence, should have retreated as far as he conveniently or safely can, to avoid the violence of the assault, before he turns upon his assailant.'... *Id.* at 184-85. In earlier days, an excusable homicide did not justify an acquittal, because *some*, even if not complete, blame attached to the slayer. Upon conviction, the defendant would escape bodily punishment and was entitled to bail, but his goods were forfeit unless and until he was pardoned by the king. In time, the pardons became issued routinely by the chancellor, and, eventually, the defendant was simply acquitted, in the same manner as the perpetrator of a justifiable homicide. *See* EDWARD H. EAST, 1 PLEAS OF THE CROWN at 220 (1806). Foster attributes the change to the statute of 24 Henry 8, c. 5. MICHAEL FOSTER, CROWN CASES at 275 (3d ed. 1809). To that practical extent, the two forms of defense—justifiable and excusable homicide—merged; they did not merge, however, with respect to the duty to retreat in an effort to avoid the need for deadly force. That issue, initially germane only with respect to what formerly was an excusable

Appendix

homicide, remained a focal point of debate and, to some extent, remains so today.

The views expressed by Blackstone are consistent with those stated by East, Hawkins, Hale, and Foster. See EAST, *supra*, 219-22; WILLIAM HAWKINS, 1 PLEAS OF THE CROWN 79-88 (John Curwood ed., 8th ed. 1824); MATTHEW HALE, 1 HISTORY OF THE PLEAS OF THE CROWN 478-92 (1847); FOSTER, *supra*, 273-78. Thus, Foster wrote: 'In the case of justifiable self-defence the injured party may repel force by force in defence of his person, habitation, or property, against one who manifestly intendeth and endeavoureth by violence or surprize to commit a known felony upon either. In these cases he is not obliged to retreat, but may pursue his adversary *till he findeth himself out of danger,* and if in a conflict between them he happeneth to kill, such killing is justifiable.' FOSTER, *supra*, at 273 (emphasis added). On the other hand: 'He therefore who, in the case of mutual conflict, would excuse himself upon the foot of self-defence must shew, that before a mortal stroke given he had declined any farther combat and retreated as far as he could with safety; and also that he killed his adversary through mere necessity, and to avoid immediate death. If he faileth in either of these circumstances he will incur the penalties of manslaughter.' *Id.* at 277. As Wharton noted, when these two rules were construed with relation to each other, **the duty of an assaulted person to retreat seemed to depend on whether killing the assailant**

Stand Your Ground —
TO KILL, OR NOT TO KILL...

under the circumstances would be justifiable or merely excusable. If the former, there was no duty to retreat; if the latter, there was. FRANCIS WHARTON, THE LAW OF HOMICIDE, § 291 (Frank H. Bowlby ed., 3d ed.1907). Beale took issue with that approach. Though acknowledging that the line between the authority to stand one's ground and the duty to retreat to avoid the necessity of killing was consistent with the distinction in the old law between justifiable and excusable homicides—between homicides committed in execution of the law and those committed in private defense—Beale asserted that Foster failed, in the case of an excusable homicide, to distinguish between the function of retreat as a means of avoiding the need to kill, and its function to avoid responsibility for the combat, and that, in effect, he blurred the distinctions between justifiable and excusable homicides. Joseph H. Beale, Jr., *Retreat from a Murderous Assault*, 16 HARV. L.REV. 567, 575-76 (1903). Noting a split of authority in the United States on whether, generally, a person under attack by another may stand his ground and resist with deadly force or must retreat if retreat is possible, Beale took as the prevailing rule that 'there is no need of retreat, but the assailed may kill the assailant if it is otherwise necessary to save his own life,' that 'if retreat would not (so far as the assailant can see) diminish the danger, he may defend himself on the spot,' and that 'if one is assailed in his own dwellinghouse, which is his castle, he is not obliged to withdraw therefrom and leave himself in that respect defenseless.' *Id.* at 579. He urged, however,

Appendix

that no killing that is not necessary can be justified, that it is not necessary to kill in self-defense when the person under attack can defend himself/ herself by withdrawing, and that '[t]he only property which the law permits him to protect by killing a wrongdoer is his dwellinghouse, and that only when its protection is necessary to the safety of his person.' *Id.* At 580-81. Perkins and Boyce, writing in 1982, favored Foster's view, rather than that of Beale. They regarded the majority American view to be that a blameless person who is the subject of a 'murderous assault' may stand his or her ground and use deadly force if reasonably necessary to save himself/herself. They acknowledged, however, that a substantial minority of jurisdictions had adopted the view that even an innocent victim of a murderous assault must elect an obviously safe retreat, if available, rather than resort to deadly force, unless (1) the victim is in his/her home at the time, (2) the assailant is one he/she is lawfully attempting to arrest, or (3) the assailant is a robber. *See* ROLLIN PERKINS AND RONALD BOYCE, CRIMINAL LAW 1119-37 (3d ed.1982). *See also Self-Help: Extrajudicial Rights, Privileges and Remedies in Contemporary American Society,* 37 Vand. L.Rev. 845, 882-83 (1984) noting the split of authority on whether deadly force may be used without safe retreat but asserting that '[b]ecause a successful retreat prevents harm to both aggressors and defenders, a duty to retreat before the use of deadly force seems to be a desirable limitation on the privilege of self defense')." (bold added for emphasis)

www.ingramcontent.com/pod-product-compliance
Lightning Source LLC
Chambersburg PA
CBHW050639300426
44112CB00012B/1865